ACKNOWLEL

The author always gets the credit for the success of a book, but every book involves many people with expertise in a variety of areas. This is especially true when the project includes a DVD. It gives me great pleasure to thank all those who have contributed to *Couture Sewing: The Couture Skirt*.

I would especially like to thank Louise Passey, Linda Homan, Derek Piazza, and Audrah Davidson, who made the many samples for the DVD; Judy Neukam and Gary Junken for their suggestions and help during filming; Robin Denning for her outstanding editorial contribution; and Liam Goodman for the book photography. I would also like to thank Fred Dennis, Margaret Duffy, Nancy Erickson, Lourdes Font, Kevin Jones, Anne Kendall, Harold Koda, Joy Landeira, Julie Le, Timothy Long, Phyllis Magidson, Hazel Matthys, McCall Pattern Co., Bob Purcell, the late Elizabeth Rhodes, Dennita Sewell, Carole and Leslie Walker, as well as members of the VintageFashionGuild.org and my students, who have provided information, encouragement, and inspiration.

I particularly appreciate the support of Amann-Mettler, Apple Annie, Bernina USA, Britex Fabrics, Linton Tweeds, Redfern Enterprises and Eurosteam Irons, Sawyer Brook Fabrics, and Superior Threads for providing materials, supplies, and equipment for this project.

I am particularly grateful to The Taunton Press for undertaking this challenging project and the many people who helped to make it successful. I would like to thank my editor, Shawna Mullen; the video team—Judy Neukam (technical editor), Evamarie Gomez (producer), and Gary Junken (videographer); the book team—Lynne Phillips (layout and production manager), Nora Fuentes (editorial production manager), Betty Christiansen (copy editor), Liam Goodman (photographer), Erin Giunta (photo editor), Angela Hastings (stylist), Tim Stobierski (assistant book editor), and Rosalind Loeb Wanke (art director).

Thanks also to the following institutions and their staffs during many years of research: the Art Institute of Chicago; Museum of Fine Arts, Boston; Brooklyn Museum; Chicago History Museum; Costume Institute of the Metropolitan Museum of Art; Edward C. Blum Design Laboratory at the Fashion Institute of Technology; Fashion Institute of Design and Merchandising, Los Angeles; Special Collections at the Fashion Institute of Technology; Fine Arts Museum of San Francisco; the Irene Lewisohn Costume Reference Library; Kent State University Museum; Lake Blackshear Regional Library, Americus, Georgia; Los Angeles County Museum of Art; Museum of the City of New York; Phoenix Art Museum; Powerhouse Museum, Sydney, Australia; Royal Ontario Museum; National Museum of American History at the Smithsonian Institution; Stephens College; Texas Fashion Collection at the University of North Texas; and the Victoria and Albert Museum.

Lastly, I am grateful to my grandmother, the late Lottie Davis Sumner, who taught me how to sew; to my mother, the late Juanita Sumner Brightwell, who taught me to always do my best; and to my husband, Charlie W. Shaeffer, for his continued support and encouragement.

CONTENTS

The fabric used to make this skirt from 1967 has a subtle plaid woven into the wool with mohair. The front faux wrap is faced with the same turquoise silk used in the blouse to create a luxurious and unique ensemble with the matching jacket.

INTRODUCTION

When I look at Chanel skirts, I have a vision of Coco
Chanel walking hurriedly from one place to another
on the streets of Paris. The skirts have many different
styles, but the faux wrap is one of the most popular.
And one thing all of the skirts have in common is
that they allow the wearer to walk easily without
restriction. When I began collecting Chanel couture
pieces, I became fascinated with more than just how
they were made. As a collector, I have spent nearly
as much time dating the more than 75 Chanel
originals and copies I own as I have examining their
structure and design. My collection encompasses
Chanel's Comeback years (1954–1971), what I
call the In-Between years (1971–1983), and the
Lagerfeld years (1983–present). Without access
to Chanel archives—which are not open to the
public—I was able to date my collection using
other methods.

I made this brown and black tweed skirt using techniques shown in this book and the accompanying DVD. The silk lining extends to the edges; the underlap is trimmed out in the stomach area but extends to the side front below that. The waist darts were eased into the waistband. I can dress this up or down and wear it almost anywhere!

Looking through back issues of *Vogue, Harper's Bazaar,* and *Elle* for photographs of suits, I was first able to precisely date one photographed by *Vogue* in 1960, and so it began. The earliest suit I have was pictured on the cover of *Elle* in 1957. If you have never looked at an original Chanel garment, beneath the Chanel label there is a tape—the bolduc—with a reference number on it. These numbers point to records of the date purchased, the number of hours required to make the garment, and details about the fabrics, trims, and notions used to make it as well as the workroom where it was made. Over time, I have been able to associate bolduc numbers as low as 05600 to 1957, up to the 81500 series made in 2003. I may never know all the details about my vintage pieces or those I have examined in museums, but the mystery only fuels my imagination. In the pages that follow, we will sew the couture skirt using techniques I have developed through decades of research, practice, and teaching. I hope you will join me.

CHAPTER ONE

Getting Started

If you want to go all out with bold fabric, trims, and details, you can find lots of inspiration from vintage Chanel pieces. This eye-catching skirt from 1965 is trimmed with a selvage edge that was then embellished with chenille yarn, and the buttons are hand painted.

DESIGN AND MATERIALS

Before we sew, we plan. And, for many of us, the planning is as enjoyable as the sewing. It is our love of textiles, beauty, and craftsmanship that spurs us to develop fine sewing skills. Deciding how to quilt and trim your couture skirt may be as simple as creating a skirt to match a jacket already in your wardrobe. Or, perhaps this skirt is destined to be worn as a separate, and you are looking for ideas to construct and trim it. Whether you have found luxurious trims for purchase or have chosen to work with self-fabric, a crochet hook, and your imagination, you can create a one-of-a-kind couture skirt that expresses your personality, taste, and style. Let's get started!

Chanel's skirts were just the right length—not too short nor too long—and designed for easy movement.

FABRICS

You may, of course, sew a skirt from any fabric you like, and when sewing a couture skirt, the possibilities are vast. Because we will take the time to stabilize, interface, and often quilt the fabric, even very soft or unstable fabrics can be used quite successfully. For the lining, silk is my favorite fabric, because it is easier to work with than polyester, nylon, or rayon. It can be crepe, China silk, habutai, or charmeuse.

1. This is the fabric I am working with. The grain is easy to see and the overall pattern is simple, making it easy to quilt. You can place the quilt lines as close together or as far apart as you like.

2. The fabric shown at left is a very lightweight voile that will improve if you quilt it. I would quilt this along the gold thread here. That's a little far apart for the lightness of the voile, so it will hang softly.

3. Look at this beautiful plaid. It could be worn with a solid jacket or a matching jacket. It is easier to quilt vertical lines, but you could quilt it horizontally or even in rectangles. You might choose to quilt along the narrow or the wide color bars.

4. The design on this fabric is couched wool on top of wool fabric. You could machine-quilt this following the outline of the couching, or you could hand-quilt it. Very few Chanel skirts and jackets are hand-quilted, but this fabric would be an ideal choice if you wanted to do hand quilting.

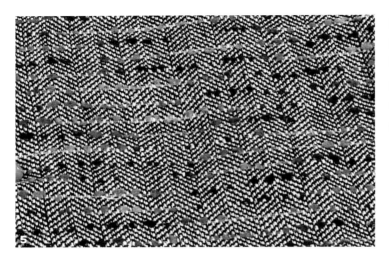

5. At first glance, this fabric's horizontal design calls for horizontal quilting. Upon closer inspection, this is a herringbone weave, and you could quilt vertically using the herringbone lines as a guide.

6. This is another fabric that could easily be quilted either horizontally or vertically because of the pattern of the fabric. You simply have to choose— which do you want to emphasize?

7. Here it is very obvious that you would quilt in a horizontal pattern. It would be nice in a skirt, because you only have to match the stripes in one seam at the center back.

LINING AND TRIMS

For the lining, I always prefer a lightweight silk (such as the silk charmeuse I'm using for the skirt in this book), a lightweight silk crepe, or plain-weave silk like China silk, but I recognize that there are some very good rayon linings today. Silk is warmer in winter, cooler in warm weather, and easier to sew.

Many times, a skirt is part of an ensemble, and it may or may not be embellished with trim. On the skirt I'm making, there will be no trim because I plan to wear it with two different jackets made from the same fabric, and each jacket is trimmed differently. However, many skirts do feature trim. Whether festive or subtle, feel free to use trim to exercise your creativity. Here are some ideas.

1. On the skirt I am making, I am not going to put on a trim. I'm going to wear this skirt with two jackets that have different trims, and this is one of them. It has a ribbon barely visible beneath the trim to give it a frame.

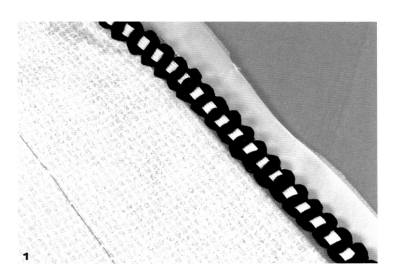

2. The other jacket I made with this pink fabric has a trim I made using the selvage and gimp. The fringe from the selvage shows on both sides, under the gimp. To stack the selvages and gimp, sew the selvage fringe at the outside edge, then place the gimp on it to determine where the inside selvage will be placed. Remove the gimp and place the selvage on the inside edge. (Instead of selvage, you might also consider a purchased piping or a piping you have made from the lining fabric.)

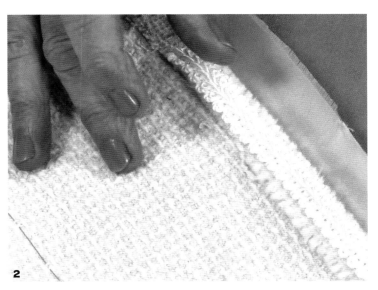

3. This fringe is a selvage edge in brown and cream, which is inserted like a piping under the finished edge. I would sew it by hand, then I would finish the lining.

4. A plain selvage piping provides a more tailored look.

5. And this selvage has a short fringe with a little sparkle in it.

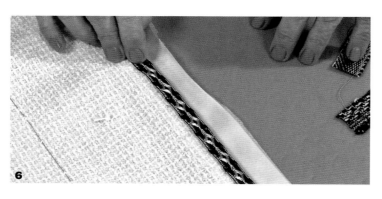

6. If you're going to sew a trim on top of the fabric, sew by hand, then finish the lining. With this in mind, you can remove the trim easily and replace it if it is soiled or you want to change the look of the design.

7. This simple trim is a strip of self-fabric cut on the bias, fringed, and finished with gimp, ribbon, or soutache on top.

TIP The most important consideration when selecting trims is that they should be as lightweight and soft as possible. I encourage you to experiment to create original trims.

COUTURE COLLECTION

This turquoise green and black plaid skirt features vertical slot seams with black underlays on the front. The black trim at the top of the skirt is a faced band. This straight skirt's seams are on the side front and side back, with a zipper on the left hip and quilting every 3 ¾ in.

CHAPTER TWO

The Pattern

This skirt is one of
the pink bouclé
samples seen in the
accompanying DVD.
One of the samples
is smaller; however,
this one is made to
my measurements.
I will enjoy wearing it
with either of my two
pink bouclé jackets.

A PERFECT PATTERN

Part of the appeal of this couture skirt is the simplicity of the design. It is a straight skirt with overlapping front panels that move freely while you are walking. This design feature can be added easily to any commercial pattern for a straight skirt. It is very important to sew a muslin toile—a mockup—of the skirt pattern you plan to use. Make fitting adjustments and don't be afraid to sew multiple muslin mockups until you are satisfied with the fit. Once fitted, the hem will hang level and the side seams will hang straight. Using your perfect pattern, let me guide you through the steps to eliminate the side seam and add the front overlap to the pattern.

A favorite Chanel idiom was "One can grow accustomed to ugliness but never to carelessness."

MAKING THE PATTERN

You will start with your altered pattern. After you have perfected the fit in your muslin toile (use a plumb line to locate the wrap position; see step 5), transfer the adjustments back to the paper pattern. Using that as the basis, make the changes needed to create the faux wrap skirt pattern.

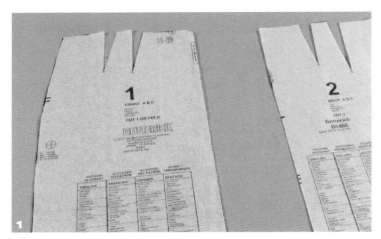

1. Start by trimming away the seam and hem allowances and the darts. Mark all notches on the seamlines. To be sure that the skirt has no flare, measure and compare the distances between the side seams and the center seams, in more than one place below the hip.

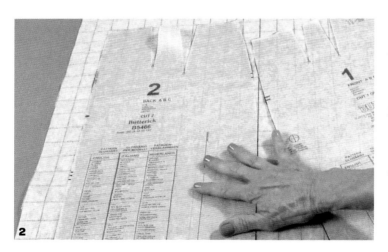

2. We will create the new pattern on pattern cloth with a grid. Draw a vertical line to represent the side seam. Place the pattern pieces on top of the pattern cloth so the side seams are aligned with the vertical line. Leave several inches at center front for the addition of the wrap.

3. With the elimination of the side seam, a dart is created at the side.

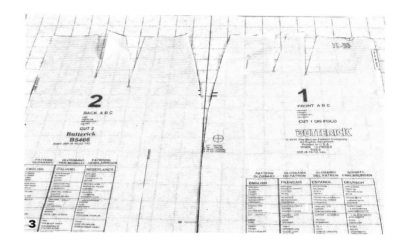

4. Pin the pattern to the pattern cloth and draw all the seamlines onto the pattern cloth. Mark center front and the hemline.

TIP Use a soft pencil to draw on the pattern cloth. A soft lead will mark more easily than a hard lead. Experiment with the point on the pencil—if it is too sharp, it may snag on the pattern cloth. Just dull the point a bit for better results.

5. Determine the width of the wrap. By working with the muslin toile and a plumb line, I located the wrap position. The wrap can extend as far toward the side seam as you like.

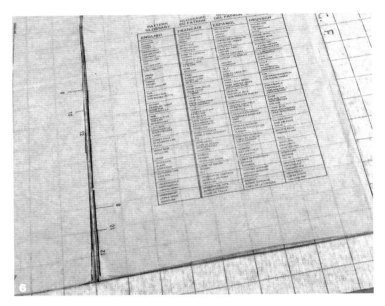

6. On the pattern cloth, draw the edge of the wrap parallel to the center front. Locate it the desired distance from the center front. Extend the hemline to the edge of the wrap.

7. To mark the waistline on the wrap, place the original tissue pattern face-down on the wrap portion. Align the center front, then trace the seamline at the waist.

HOW MUCH FABRIC WILL I NEED?

Measure the width of the new pattern piece and add at least 2 in. to account for two 1-in. seam allowances. Most bouclés are 50 in. to 60 in. wide. Knee-length skirts are generally less than 24 in. long, so it may be possible to cut both skirt pieces from less than a yard of fabric depending on your hip size and the overlap amount. For larger sizes, plan on using two lengths—about 1¾ yd. Since the lining fabric is 42–45 in. wide, all sizes will need two lengths of lining. Measure your pattern for precise yardage requirements.

COUTURE
COLLECTION

What appears to be a blouse and skirt is really a dress. The skirt was made separately and then sewn to the blouse. There are tucks on the inside of the skirt to create the flare. The center back panel is underlined with cotton batiste, and the center front is trimmed subtly with a selvage edge.

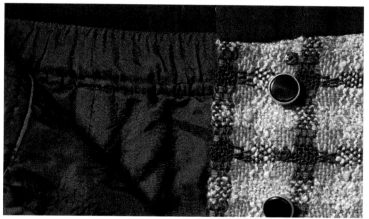

The skirt lining extends to the top of the waistband.

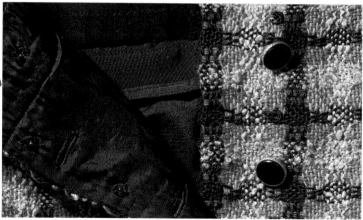

When the stitching along the top of the waistband is removed, the grosgrain ribbon can be seen.

CHAPTER THREE

Layout and Marking

To make the 3½-in.-wide waistband, twice that amount of fabric was prepared by tucking out the tan stripes to create solid red. Lighter colors advance and darker colors recede—this is a good example of how the principle works to flatter the figure, and how to use a horizontal-striped fabric successfully.

MARKING
THE FABRIC

Before the first cut and before the first stitch, take a moment to study the fabric. Is it hard to tell the difference between the right side and the wrong side? Does the fabric have a subtle nap that could be noticed after the skirt is finished? Now is the time to decide whether stripes or plaids need to be matched. Next is the marking. Everything from the positions of darts and notches to the placement of quilting lines will be marked before beginning to sew. Until the fabric starts to look like a skirt, the markings will be valuable reference points. Take the time to lay out and mark the pattern pieces accurately, and you will be glad you did.

Chanel was a design pioneer and one of the first to move away from corsets and long, cumbersome skirts.

HOW TO LAY OUT THE PATTERN

Cut rectangles of fabric a few inches wider and longer than each pattern piece and work with each section individually while laying out the pattern. Check the right side and the wrong side of the fabric, as well as the nap. Orient all pieces so that the top of the skirt is consistently placed at the top of the fabric.

1. Spread the fabric right side up and mark the top right corner with a cross-stitch. This is a reminder to place the skirt tops toward the top right consistently, and a reminder of which side is the right side of the fabric.

2. Use basting cotton to thread-trace markings onto the fabric. Basting cotton breaks easily during removal, so it does not disturb machine stitches when you pull it out.

3. Place the pattern at least 1 in. from the raw edge. Mark the grainline at center front with a pin.

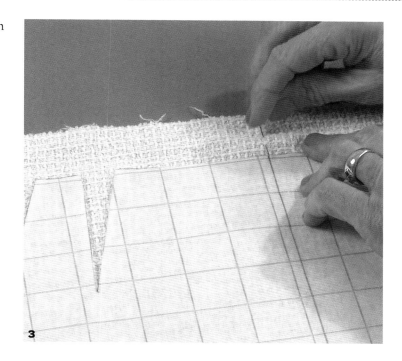

4. Use pins to hold the pattern in place. Place pins parallel to the grainline.

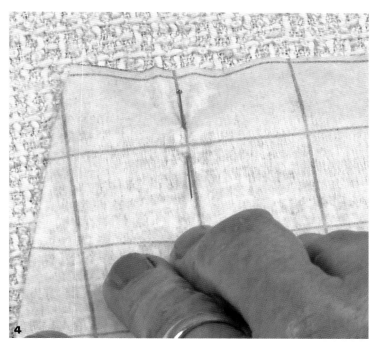

MARKING

When marking the fabric, you are marking the locations of seamlines. This will ensure precise construction of the skirt you previously adjusted during the fitting of the muslin toile.

1. Mark the seamlines by thread-tracing along the edges of the pattern pieces. To mark the corners precisely, insert the needle into the corner and take a ½-in. stitch. Then insert the needle ½ in. before the beginning of the adjacent seamline, bringing it out exactly at the corner.

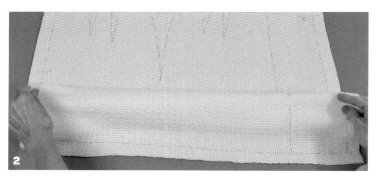

2. In addition to the seamlines, mark darts, notches, the bottom of the zipper, the dart center on the side, and the hem. Mark the left front rectangle on the underlap over the stomach.

3. Baste a row 2 in. above the hem to mark the bottom of the quilting.

MARKING THE QUILT LINES

By the time you mark the quilt lines, you have a lot of thread tracings. To avoid confusion, switch to a different stitch or thread color so that you can easily identify the quilt lines when you machine-stitch.

1. Determine the placement of the quilt lines at center front and center back first. Pin. Then determine the placement at the side. Fill in the remaining quilt lines.

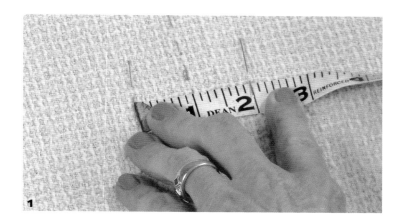

2. Continue marking quilt lines using a cardboard gauge—it's easier than using a tape measure. Pin.

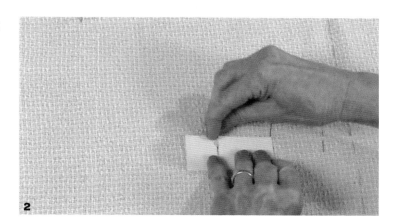

3. To differentiate the quilt lines from other markings, use a different stitch or thread color. I used an uneven basting stitch on the quilt lines.

MARKING THE LINING

The skirt lining is silk charmeuse, and I'm using the matte side of the fabric since the shiny side does not photograph well. The markings are made with a sharp pencil on the wrong side of the lining— the side that will not show when the skirt is finished.

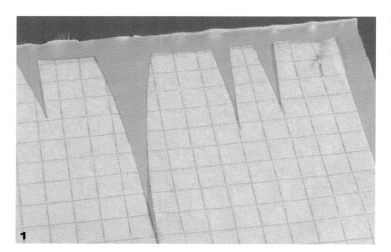

1. Cut two rectangles of silk fabric the same size as the skirt pieces.

2. The only seam that needs to be marked is at the waist. Mark with a sharp pencil. Because I marked on the wrong side of the lining, the pencil marks will be hidden.

COUTURE COLLECTION

Consider the nap when laying out and cutting the skirt. As you move your hand back and forth across the fabric, feel for differences in one direction versus the other. When there is a nap, it will feel smoother in one direction, and more resistant in the opposite direction. Orient the fabric so the smooth side is running from top to bottom on all pattern pieces. At right, the fabric is a blend of wool with mohair running through to create a subtle plaid. It may not look like it, but there is a distinct nap and pattern in the fabric.

CHAPTER FOUR

Shaping the Skirt

The contrast between the navy and white makes it easy to see the shaping at the sides of the waist. Notice how the size of the navy bars stays consistent while the white background gets narrower toward the waist. The shaping at the waist can be accomplished with easing only, or a combination of easing and darts or seams.

EASING AND SHAPING

Taking flat fabric and turning it into a three-dimensional article of clothing is the joy of dressmaking and tailoring. We generally achieve garment shaping using curved seams, darts, pleats, or gathers. When making the couture skirt, the fabric is molded and manipulated with heat and steam. Responding to the will of the maker, the elegant shape of the skirt emerges. Through carefully considered methods, we will craft a one-of-a-kind couture skirt.

The Chanel look appealed to American women who wanted suits that were understated but elegant.

THE RIGHT TOOLS

Whether you are a beginner or very skilled, the difference between frustration and success can often be attributed to using the right tools. As you come to understand why these tools are chosen, this knowledge can be applied to all kinds of sewing situations.

1

1. Use a sharp needle such as a Microtex or a needle made for sewing jeans. A universal needle, while not quite as sharp, will work on many fabrics.

2

2. The right presser foot helps with stitching through multiple bulky layers. Try a straight stitch foot or a ¼-in. quilting foot like these.

3. The bobbin thread will be pulled to gather the fabric, so use a strong thread made from polyester or silk.

NOTE For demonstration purposes, I use contrasting thread so it can be seen easily.

3

4. Set the stitch length at 3 mm or 8 stitches per inch. Use a longer stitch length for heavier fabrics. Loosen the tension on the needle thread slightly.

4

5. Some bobbin cases have a finger. Running thread through the hole at the end of the finger will increase bobbin tension slightly.

TIP Check the owner's manual for your sewing machine to learn about tension adjustments if your sewing machine is different from mine.

5

EASING

The fabric will be shaped to fit the body by easing excess fabric and then pressing it to keep the shape. Easing fabric is a matter of gathering it up to compress it into a smaller shape. The heat and steam used in pressing cause the fabric to retain the new shape.

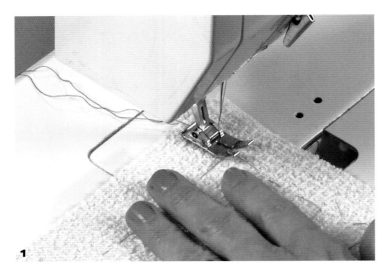

1. Begin stitching about ½ in. from the center back, with the fabric right side up. Sew right next to the thread tracing.

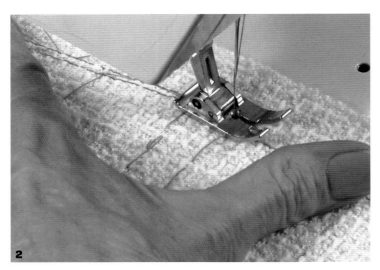

2. Stitch a second row in the seam allowance about ⅛ in. above the first row.

3. From the wrong side, pull the bobbin threads.

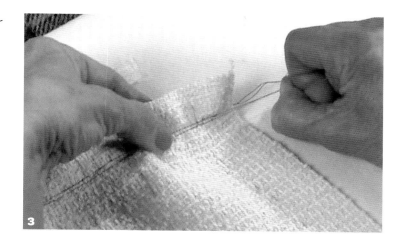

4. Rather than trying to work with a tape measure, mark the waist measurements on a length of seam binding. Use a pencil to mark the center front, the center back, and the center of the side dart. This seam binding will become a valuable tool throughout the project, so keep it handy.

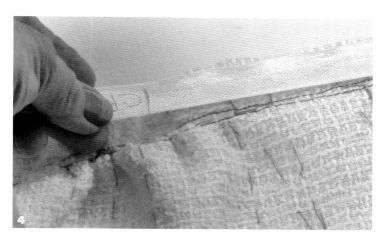

5. To better control the amount of ease, anchor the threads at the beginning of the ease stitching. Wrap the threads around a pin in a figure eight. As you pull the bobbin threads, they will remain securely attached.

NOTE Pick up a very small bit of fabric when setting the pin.

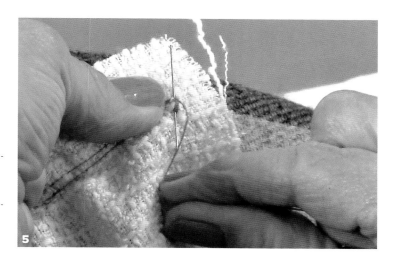

6. Crowd the fabric more in areas where fullness is needed, and less in flat areas. The area of the side dart needs the most fullness for this skirt. Press on a curved surface, such as this ham, to avoid flattening the fabric. I hold the steam iron just above the fabric, then use my hands to press and ease the fabric.

HINT Use a press cloth when pressing from the right side. Here, the press cloth is not used so you can see better.

7. Ease the lining, following the same steps to ease the skirt. The silk did not ease as well as the wool, but the fabric is soft and the fullness will not add bulk. You can also fold out small darts and sew them flat.

ALL ABOUT DARTS

A dart is an efficient way to remove excess fabric in an area to be shaped. When there is too much fabric to be eased into the section, consider sewing a small, short dart.

1. When easing is not enough to remove the fullness, you can use a small, short dart. The red thread tracing shows a dart that is shorter and narrower than the original dart. The dart will reduce the amount of easing required in this area.

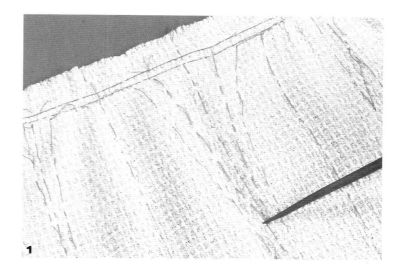

2. Begin stitching the basted dart just above the waist seamline. At the point, tie a knot. Remove the basting threads.

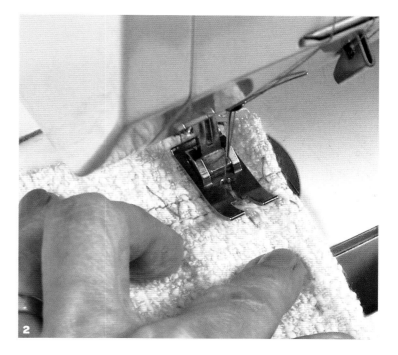

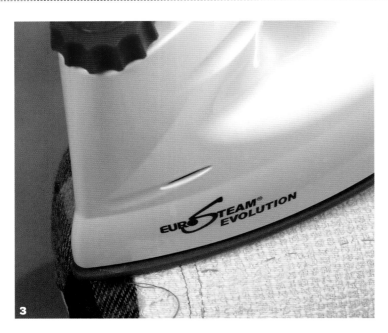

3. Press the dart flat. Then slash the dart at the center and press it open.

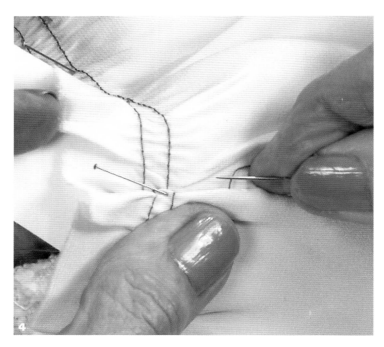

4. If you put a dart in the skirt, you'll have to put a dart in the lining. Stack the skirt and lining wrong sides together; pin them together at the waist. You'll see excess silk over the skirt dart. Fold out a corresponding dart in the lining, pin it, and sew it permanently using fell stitches.

TIP Slip a piece of cardboard between the lining and the skirt to separate the layers and prevent the needle from catching on the skirt fabric while sewing.

COUTURE COLLECTION

This vintage 1963 skirt was made to fit a woman with a 24-in. waist and 39-in. hips. The shaping to accommodate the difference is accomplished by easing the darts into the waist. On the dress form, the fullness is evident, but on the body this skirt skims the figure smoothly. There is no quilting on this skirt, and the closure is a zipper hidden under the lap trim on the left hip. This is a nice example of a Chanel skirt made from smooth silk, rather than the more common and bulkier novelty bouclé.

CHAPTER FIVE

Quilting the Skirt

As is generally the case, the vertical quilting in this skirt is not noticeable from the right side of the skirt. The machine stitching sinks into the texture of the subtle tone-on-tone plaid. Don't worry if the quilting does show. The quilting was a status symbol that indicated you had purchased an original Chanel instead of a copy.

QUILTING AND STABILIZING

Of all the characteristics associated with Chanel, perhaps none is more distinctive than the quilting of the fabric to the lining. It is hard to appreciate just how cozy and comfortable this fabrication is if you have never worn it. A bouclé weave is often loosely woven, lofty, and not very stable without the stabilization provided by the quilting. The stitching that joins the two fabrics is usually placed in vertical rows a couple of inches apart, although horizontal lines of quilting and other formations can be found. Careful consideration in the planning stages will pay off in the durability and appearance of the skirt.

Chanel believed that simplicity is the key to elegance.

WHERE AND HOW TO QUILT

Quilting on a skirt is performed after easing in the shape and before assembling the pieces. The fabric is quilted to the lining. The permanent quilt stitching is usually sewn by machine, although hand quilting is an option when the appearance of machine stitching would interrupt the fabric design and mar its beauty.

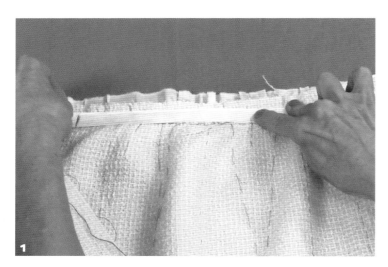

1. Stack the fabric and lining sections together and align the center back, center of side dart, and center front. Pin. Use the marked seam binding to measure the waistline. Adjust if necessary.

TIP Spread the fabric on a table so it won't wrinkle, and so you can prop your arms on the edge of the table to sew (so you won't tire). Always remember: If you don't get a wrinkle in, you won't have to get a wrinkle out.

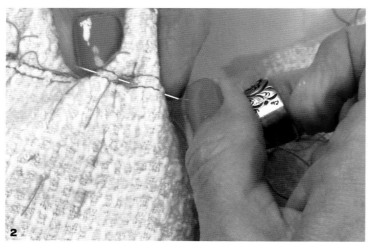

2. Using a long needle and basting thread, sew along the waistline with a long running stitch.

3. Pin the fabric and lining together between the thread-traced quilting lines.

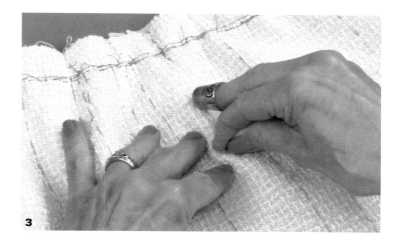

4. From the right side, baste over the quilting lines with a short needle and diagonal stitches.

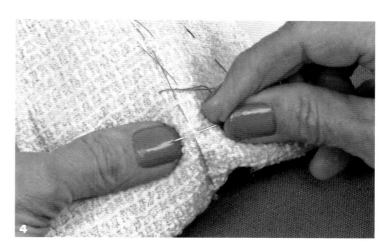

5. Set the machine for 4 mm or 6 stitches per inch. Beginning with a row in the center of the skirt, stitch from the seamline at the waist to the basted line 2 in. above the hem. Roll the skirt up so it will fit under the arm of the machine.

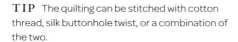

TIP The quilting can be stitched with cotton thread, silk buttonhole twist, or a combination of the two.

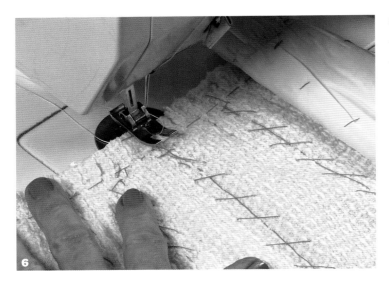

6. Stitch all rows to the right, then return to center and stitch all rows to the left.

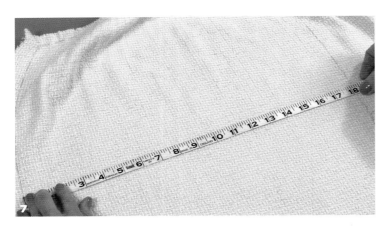

7. Pull the quilting thread tails in between the layers with a crochet hook or calyx-eye needle. Give the threads a sharp tug to remove any slack and knot the ends. Remove the basting threads and measure the skirt to see whether the width was affected by the quilting process. Adjust if necessary. Give the skirt sections a light press before stabilizing the front edges.

STABILIZING

Stabilizing is important for the function and the appearance of the garment. There are many ways to reinforce edges and stabilize the fabric to hold up to the stress of fasteners and wear. Stabilization will cause the front overlapping panels to hang straight, despite the light weight of the fabric. To stabilize the front edges of the skirt use a stay. Use a selvage of any lightweight silk, such as organza or the lining fabric. You can also use seam binding or a torn strip of silk. Remove all stretch from the stay by wetting it and then pressing it.

1. Establish the length of the stay for the front edge of the overlap. Measure the pattern from the waist to the hem. Mark this length on the stay with a pencil. On the overlap, pin the stay at the waist and at the hem. On the underlap stay, mark the base of the rectangle. The fabric may have already stretched a little. This is not uncommon, and some fabrics will stretch quite a lot depending on the fiber and weave.

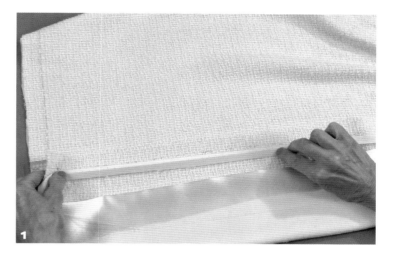

2. To finish the edge of the overlap, ease the fabric to the stay. Pin the center, and then divide the spaces and add other pins to ease the edge. Baste the stay into place using a long needle and long running stitches.

TIP Place a ruler behind the fabric when you are pinning a single layer. The ruler separates the layers to prevent the pins from catching into the fabric below.

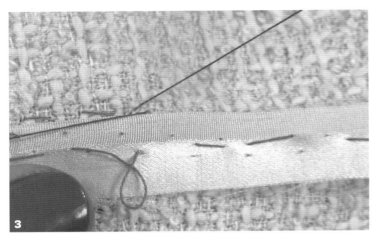

3. Sew the stay permanently at the seamline using catchstitches, demonstrated in contrasting red thread here. Trim the seam allowance to ½ in. wide and fold to the wrong side. Baste it in place.

NOTE If the edge has a trim, sew it now before the lining is sewn.

4. To finish the front edge of the underlap, trim the seam allowance to ½ in. wide and fold it to the wrong side. Baste in place. Begin about 2 in. above the hemline because the hem will be finished later. Stop at the rectangle. Press the edges on both the right side and left side. Use catchstitches to sew the edges of the seam allowances permanently.

HINT Unlike most stitches, the catchstitch is made from left to right, if you are right-handed, or right to left, if you are left-handed.

----

5. Now is a good time to finish the edge on the underlap. First, remove the fabric from the rectangle to reduce the bulk over the stomach. Next, trim about ⅜ in. above the basted line. Do not trim the lining. If you haven't already, cut off the stay at the bottom of the rectangle.

6. Turn in the lining at the edges of the overlap and underlap so that the fold is about ¹⁄₁₆ in. from the edge, and pin it. Baste it in place, then use fell stitches or slipstitches to sew it permanently. Start about 2 in. from the hemline so you can hem the skirt later.

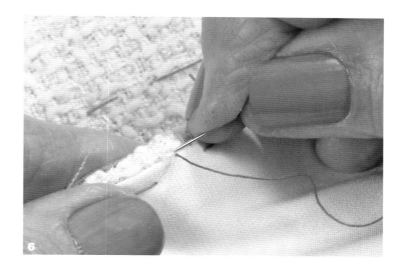

COUTURE COLLECTION

Made in the late 1960s, this red and gold plaid skirt has a facing that has been machine-stitched to simulate a waistband. The quilting is done on both sides of the gold stripes and through the centers of the red squares. The quilting appears only on the center front and center back panels.

CHAPTER SIX

Assembling

This straight skirt has a faux wrap in the front, lined in fuchsia. The lining extends to the edge of the skirt, with a single seam at center back, and waist darts have been eased into the binding on the waistband.

ASSEMBLING
THE SKIRT

An important element of the Chanel skirt is its simplicity. My design for this couture skirt takes inspiration from the many Chanel skirts in my collection. It features a single seam at center back with a zipper, and walking ease is provided by the faux wrap front. A wrap skirt made from bouclé may sound too bulky at first, but the design cleverly reduces bulk below the waist in the front. The movement of the overlap while walking makes for a flattering silhouette on many different figure types. Simple does not necessarily mean fast, as you will see, but if you take the assembly one step at a time, you will find the process to be quite logical. Sewing by hand takes time, but with practice, it gets faster and reduces ripping, and the beautiful results justify the effort.

The Chanel philosophy was to combine the freshness of youth with comfort and the ease of contemporary lifestyles, without sacrificing luxury.

FINISHING THE CENTER BACK SEAM

Now it's time to assemble the skirt. The right and left sides of the skirt are quilted and the stays are sewn at the front edges. This skirt has only one vertical seam—the seam at center back. At the front, the right front laps over the left and is hand-sewn in place. Make sure you have removed all bastings except those at the hemline, the center back and front, the waist, and the mark at the center of the dart at the side seams. The center back seam of the skirt is where the zipper will be inserted.

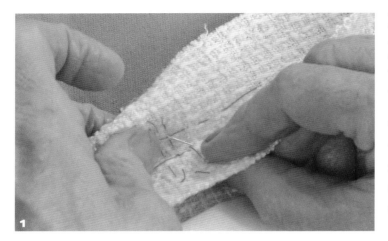

TIP Bouclé fabrics and tweeds can be bulky, and the loose weave can cause the layers to shift. That won't be a problem, however, if you baste the seam first and sew the seam in stages.

1. Pin the center back seamlines together, taking care to match the notches at the bottom of the zipper and on the seam as well as the edges at the hem.

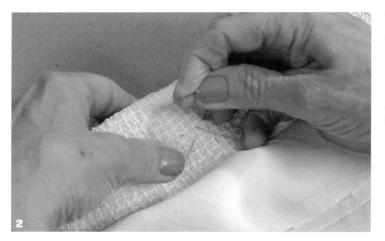

2. Start basting at the bottom of the zipper placket, the point of difficulty. Use a long needle.

NOTE I used pink embroidery floss so the basting can be seen and removed easily.

3. Once the seam is basted, remove the blue thread tracings. After the seam has been machine-stitched, it will be more difficult to remove multiple basting threads than a single thread.

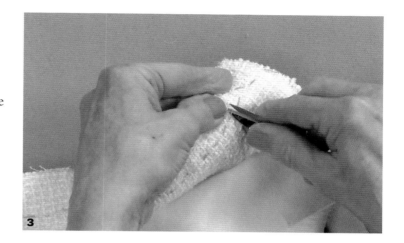

4. Use a straight stitch foot and set the stitch length to 2.5 mm or 10 stitches per inch. Begin stitching at the bottom of the zipper opening—the point of difficulty. Do not secure the beginning of the seam by backstitching, as that can cause stiffness and, if you have to rip the seam, you may leave a hole. Instead, secure the seam with a knot.

TIP When stitching, it doesn't matter which layer is on top since the seam is basted.

5. Examine the beginning of the seam at the zipper opening. If you stitched too far, remove a few stitches. If you did not stitch far enough, use a calyx-eye needle to take another stitch. A calyx-eye needle has an opening at the top, making it easy to thread the needle.

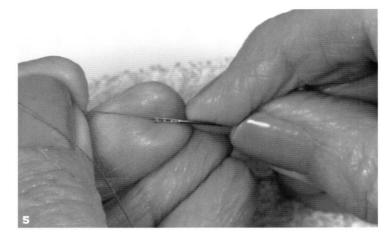

6. Pull one of the threads through to the other side and make a tailor's knot. Trim excess thread, then remove the basting stitches.

TIP On a straight seam, it is acceptable to stitch next to the basting thread so it will be easier to remove. But when stitching curved seams, always stitch on the basting for greater accuracy.

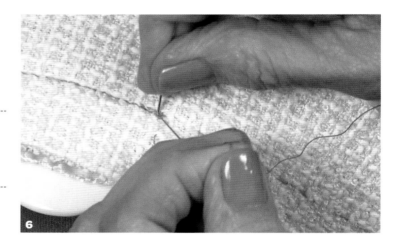

HOW TO TIE A KNOT

Use this technique to make a small knot.

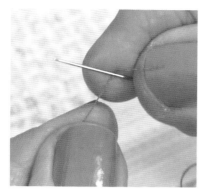

1. Thread the needle. If you are right-handed, use your right index finger to press one end of the thread against the needle while your left hand wraps it around the needle.

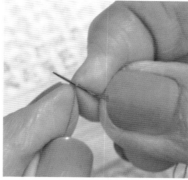

2. Wrap the thread two or three times around the needle.

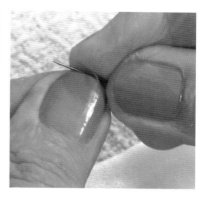

3. Using your left index finger and thumb, hold the wrapped thread in place. Transfer the needle from your right hand to your left hand. Place your left thumb at the end of the needle, at the eye of the needle, and push the needle through the wrapped thread.

4. Pull the needle with your right hand. Maintain gentle pressure on the knot with your left index finger and thumb.

5. A small knot is formed as the thread is pulled through the loops.

APPLYING THE ZIPPER STAY

Before inserting the zipper, apply stays to stabilize the opening. The zipper will not only look better, it will also be much more durable.

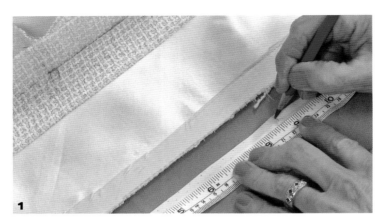

1. Cut two stays about 1 in. longer than the placket length on the pattern. Mark this length on each stay beginning about ½ in. from one end.

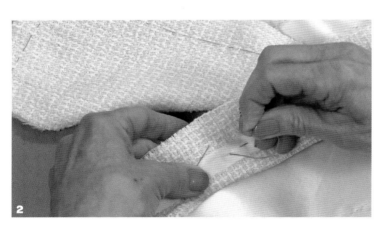

2. Pin the stay to the wrong side of the skirt with the selvage edge on the foldline. Then, baste the stay in place using a long needle.

3. Using catchstitches, attach the edge of the stay along the foldline of the zipper placket.

4. Fold the seam allowance to the wrong side. Baste about ¼ in. from the edge. Repeat these steps to stabilize the other side of the placket.

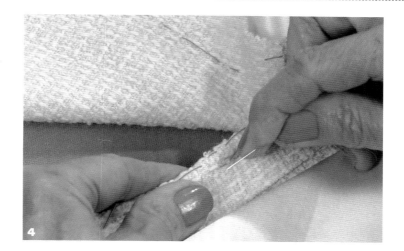

5. Press the seam and the zipper placket. The press cloth used here is a piece of the fashion fabric.

TIP Before pressing the seam, remove the basting threads. If you don't, or wait until after pressing, the threads can cause a crooked seam.

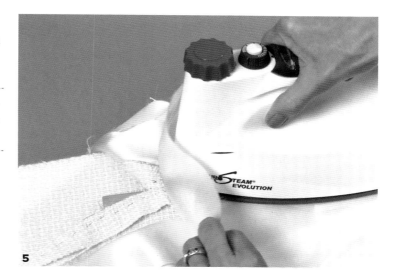

PRESSING

1. Pressing tools (clockwise): iron, ham, press cloths, sponge and water, clapper, seam stick, seam roll. The press cloths are satin-faced organza and the fashion fabric used for the skirt.

2. Pressing the seam flat sets the stitches. You might notice it is harder to unpick a seam after it has been pressed. This is because the heat and steam caused the fibers to relax and integrate with the fabric, also known as marrying the stitches. Place the organza press cloth on top of your work to protect it from the iron. Here, I am pressing without the press cloth so you can see.

3. With the wrong side up, press a seam open by placing it on a seam stick. The curved surface of the seam stick allows the fabric to drape gently toward the table during pressing. This avoids the unsightly appearance of imprinted seam allowances, which would be visible from the right side.

4. If the fabric isn't pressing well, cover it with a wooden clapper after pressing the seam. The clapper absorbs the moisture, holds the steam in the fabric, and flattens the seam. If it is really difficult to press, spank the seam with the clapper.

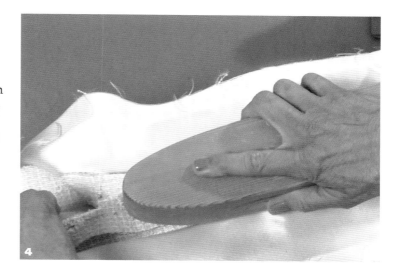

5. To get even more moisture, lightly press a damp sponge against the fabric. Here the fabric is protected by the organza press cloth. Then press with the iron.

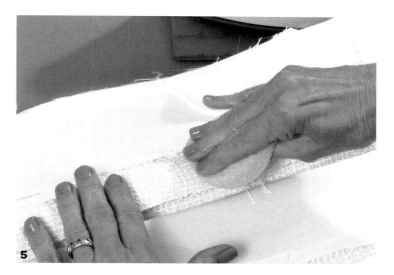

SHORTENING THE ZIPPER

How many times have you searched for a zipper in the correct color at the perfect length? You might be surprised at how common it is for a couture house to use zippers that are much longer than needed. You might also be surprised at how easy it is to shorten a zipper following these steps.

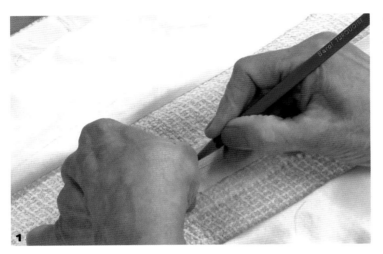

1. Use a pencil to mark the bottom of the zipper about 1 in. longer than the zipper opening. The blue basting threads at the top of the zipper mark the seamline at the waist. Align the top of the zipper so that the blue basting thread is at the waistline thread tracing on the skirt.

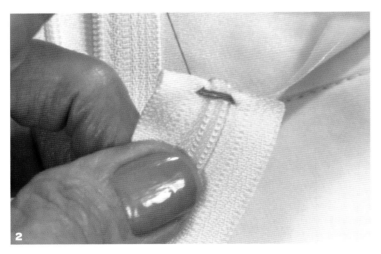

2. Sew a thread bar across the zipper coil to make a zipper stop. Cut off the excess zipper below the thread bar. Overcast the ends of the zipper tape.

HOW TO INSERT THE ZIPPER

The zipper will be inserted entirely by hand. One might expect that a hand-sewn zipper is not as strong as a machine-stitched one; however, the combination of stitches makes it very strong, especially when sewn with waxed thread. This zipper will be very secure.

1. Clip the basting at the top of the zipper, but do not remove the basting threads yet. This blue basting thread was sewn to mark the waist seamline, about ⅜ in. above the top of the zipper.

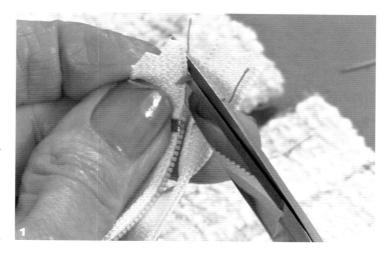

NOTE Make sure you have applied stays to the zipper plackets before inserting the zipper. Without stabilization, it's easy to stretch the edges—the finished zipper may look like a roller coaster, and it won't wear as well.

2. Align the basting threads at the top of the zipper with the thread tracing at the waistline on the skirt. Pin the zipper to the seam allowance so that you can barely see the fabric past the zipper coil.

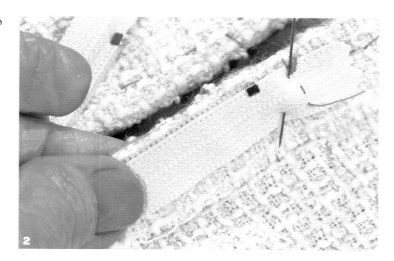

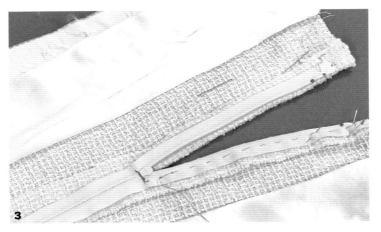

3. Using the woven line on the zipper tape as a guide, use a long needle to baste the zipper in place. Repeat on the other side.

4. When zipped, the zipper will have a slight peak where the folded edges butt together. This peak will disappear when the garment is worn.

5. Use waxed thread to sew the zipper permanently. Start about 1¼ in. below the waistline and sew toward the bottom of the zipper.

TIP Apply beeswax to make the thread stronger and tangle less. Pull the thread through beeswax, wrap it with paper towels, then press to melt the wax into the thread fibers and absorb the excess wax. I'll wax enough to sew the hooks and eyes later and wind the extra on an empty spool. See p. 74 for more details.

----

6. Sew using short running stitches that are barely visible on the right side. If you can't make the running stitches short enough, use stab stitches. I prefer running stitches to pickstitches because they allow the fabric to move with the body, and the stitches are almost invisible on the outside when finished.

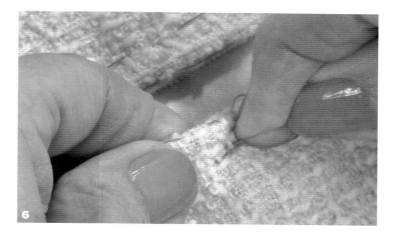

7. Stop at the bottom of the zipper pull and fasten the thread on the wrong side.

NOTE I used red thread so the stitching can be seen; however, the stitches on the right side of the fabric are so small they are almost invisible.

8. At the top of the zipper, I make small pockets to hide the zipper tab. Return to the top of the zipper and begin about 1¼ in. below the waistline seam. Sew the zipper to the seam allowance only, with running stitches next to the basting. Repeat these steps on the other side of the zipper.

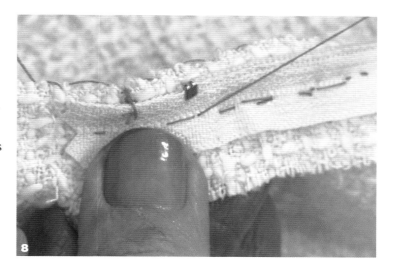

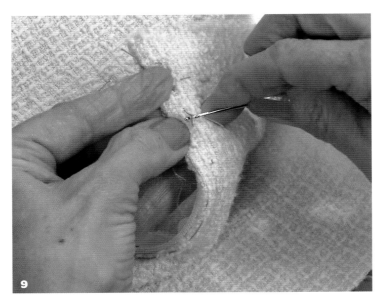

9. On the outside, remove the basting stitches. I sometimes use a very small crochet hook to remove basting threads. To finish the zipper, use very short running stitches and sew only into the top layer of fabric at the top of the zipper. This creates a small pocket and allows room for the zipper pull.

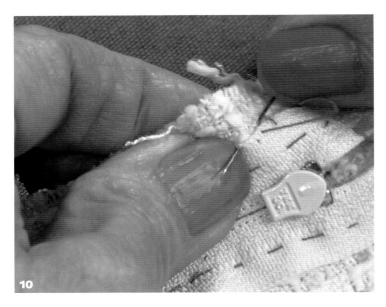

10. Use fell stitches and a short needle to secure the edges of the zipper tape to the seam allowances on unlined garments and to add security.

TIP If you are afraid the zipper won't be held securely, fold the fabric back and machine-stitch close to the fold.

---

11. Use a small rectangle of lining, with a folded edge, to cover the end of the zipper. This makes a smooth transition from the zipper to the center back seam. Sew the sides and bottom of the rectangle with running stitches.

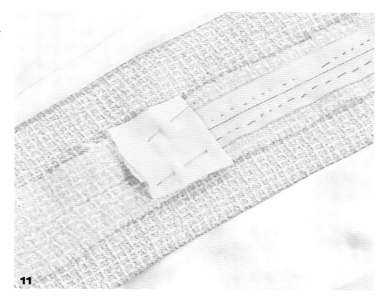

12. Sew the folded edge with fell stitches.

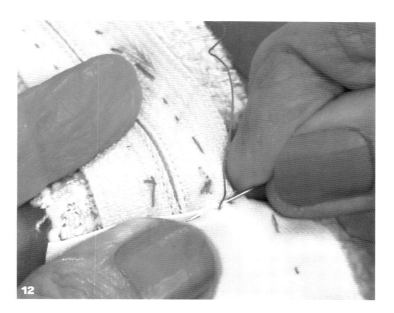

WAXED THREAD

Apply beeswax to make thread stronger and tangle less.

1. Pull the thread through a piece of beeswax.

2. Place the waxed thread on a paper towel, and cover it with another paper towel to absorb the excess wax during pressing.

3. Press with the iron as you pull the thread through the paper towels.

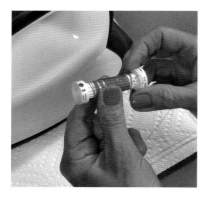

4. Make enough waxed thread for the entire project, and save it on an empty spool. You will need waxed thread for the zipper and hooks and eyes.

5. Notice how much wax is absorbed by the paper towel. You wouldn't want wax on your finished garment, so don't skip this step.

FINISHING THE LINING

Because the fabric and lining are quilted together early in the process, the edges of the lining are left loose until the skirt is assembled. Once the zipper has been inserted, the lining can be finished at the center back seam. This seam is sewn by hand so the folded edges meet, using stitches that are invisible when finished. I call this a "kissing seam."

1. Turn under the lining seam allowances on the center back seam so the folded edges meet at the seamline. At the zipper, turn under the lining a little more so it covers the stitches on the zipper tape. Baste in place.

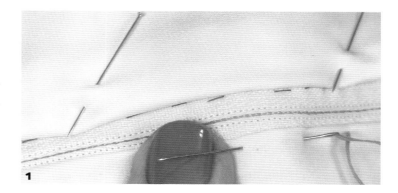

2. Starting at the center of the patch, sew the lining seam at center back. Use slipstitches to weave the needle between the folds so the stitches will be inconspicuous. Stop about 2 in. above the hemline.

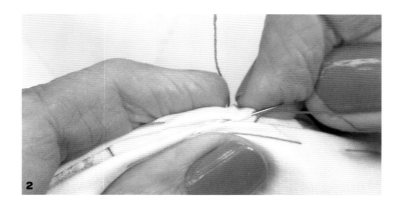

3. Starting at the top of the zipper, use slipstitches and pickstitches to sew the lining on both sides of the zipper. I prefer pickstitches, which are very small backstitches that don't go through all layers because they hold the lining flat.

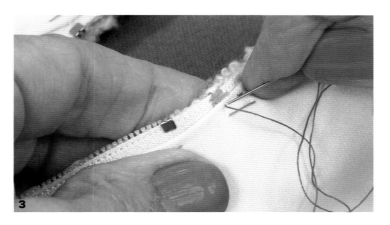

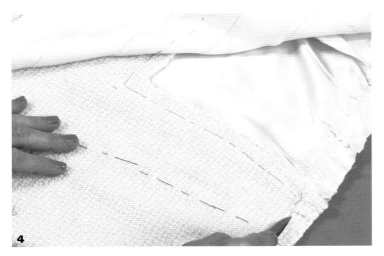

4. Now you're ready to join the skirt fronts. Arrange the right front over the left front as it will be worn. Pin the underlap along the edge of the overlap, then evaluate the amount of fashion fabric left on the underlap. You may trim away more fabric—up to 1 in. from the pinned line.

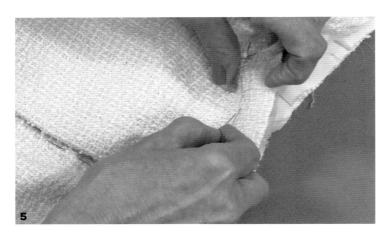

5. Align the center fronts. Pin, then baste the seamlines of the overlap and underlap together at the waist. Check the length of the waist seam against the marked seamed binding used earlier. Adjust if necessary.

6. Baste the lining and the skirt together at the waist.

COUTURE COLLECTION

While Chanel designs are known for imaginative trims and details, there are just as many iconic examples of simple, elegant designs. This salmon pink bouclé skirt has a self-fabric waistband that folds over at the top for a self-facing. From the front the straight skirt is a beautiful, simple column.

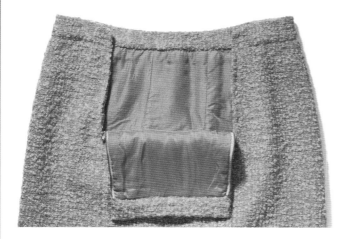

There is no center back seam; there is a center back panel with two seams and a short zipper in each seam. The two zippers facilitate dressing and accommodate the 12-in. difference between the waist and hips. The zippers are short so they don't show beneath the hem of the jacket.

CHAPTER SEVEN

The Waistband

Fabricated in a novelty wool tweed, this mid-1970s skirt was probably designed by couturiers Jean Cazaubon and Yvonne Dudel, former design assistants of Mademoiselle Chanel.

SETTING THE WAISTBAND

From barely noticeable to bold design statements, the waistbands on Chanel skirts vary from skirt to skirt. All are sewn in such a way as to minimize bulk, maximize comfort, and, of course, enhance the style of the skirt. A faced waistband is considered the traditional couture method, and it is designed to fit the waist at the bottom of the waistband. A curved waistband is nipped in to fit the waist at the top of the band. Then there are more dramatic options, such as the use of a decorative yoke made from a contrasting fabric. Any style is appropriate, whether worn with a matching jacket as part of an ensemble or allowed to shine on its own as a separate. Choose a waistband to express your style as you explore the possibilities.

A favorite Chanellism was, "Luxury must be comfortable, otherwise it is not luxury."

INTERFACING THE WAISTBAND

Inside the waistband is the structure to support the entire skirt. The interfacing is molded to fit the body and stabilizes the fabric in the waistband, so that it won't stretch out of shape.

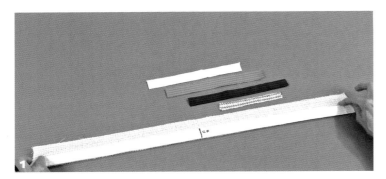

1. The waistband should be 1½ in. to 2 in. longer than the waist measurement. Use the muslin toile waistband as the pattern. For the interfacing, you have several options. Petersham (top) is used in Chanel skirts, but it isn't readily available in the United States. Use grosgrain ribbon or a polyester ribbon, or stitch two layers of hair canvas together (bottom) to interface the waistband.

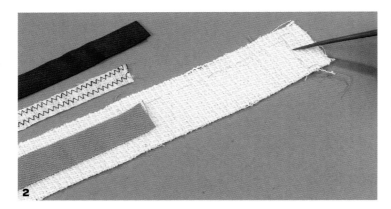

2. Mark the seamlines at the waistband center back with thread basting. This waistband on the skirt pattern is ⅝ in. wide; the waistband on my skirt is 1 in. wide—the same as the ribbon.

3. Pin the interfacing to the wrong side of the waistband, then baste the center with long diagonal stitches.

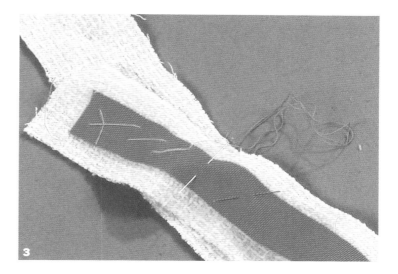

4. Fold the seam allowance over the top of the ribbon and baste about ¼ in. from the upper edge. Begin and end about ½ in. from the ends.

MITERING THE CORNER

For a clean finish with almost no bulk, miter the corners. If you haven't sewn mitered corners before, practice on scraps until your miters are perfect. Avoid unnecessary manipulation of the fabric to avoid fraying. When done well, the miter will completely enclose the cut edges of the fabric.

1. Clip the seam allowance diagonally toward the corner.

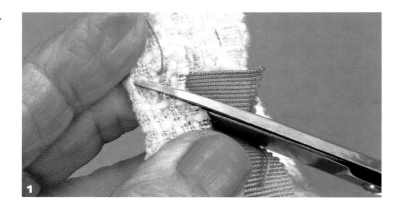

2. Fold the seam allowance diagonally at the end of the waistband. This will be folded again toward you after trimming away the excess fabric in the next step.

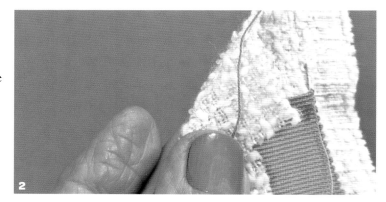

3. Trim the excess from the seam allowance at the end of the waistband.

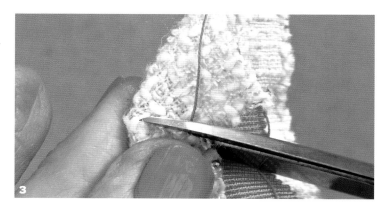

4. Butt the edges together and pin. All bulk should have been removed. Whipstitch the butted edges together.

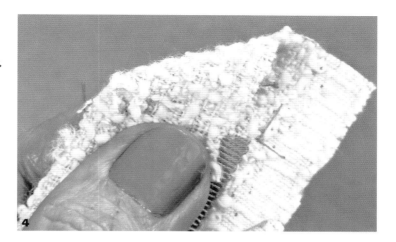

5. Fold the upper seam allowance toward you to form the mitered corner.

6. Finish the miter using fell stitches. Finish the other upper corner the same way.

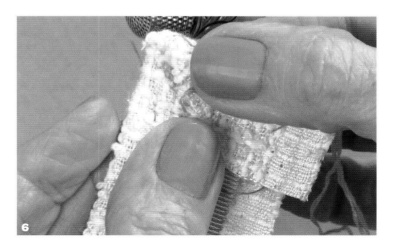

HOW TO ATTACH THE WAISTBAND

Now that the waistband has been interfaced and the edges are finished, I'm ready to sew the band to the skirt. The hooks and eyes will be sewn to the waistband before the lining is finished.

1. Pin the waistband to the skirt, aligning the center front and center back markings.

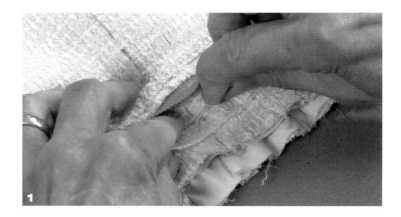

2. At center back, clip into the seam allowance of the waistband. This will allow the pieces to lie flat while machine stitching.

3. Align the side seam markings on the waistband and skirt. Baste the waistband to the skirt.

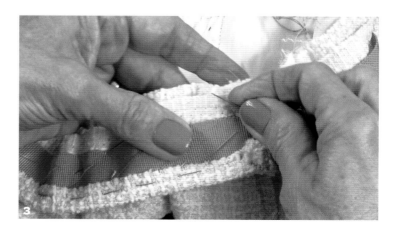

4. Machine-stitch using a straight-stitch foot.

HINT If the upper layers begin to bubble while you stitch, stitch slowly using an awl to hold the fabric firmly as it moves under the presser foot.

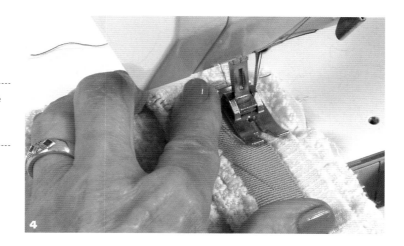

5. The machine easily stitches the seam with the notch (from step 2) allowing the fabric to lie flat. Do not backstitch to secure the seam; instead, tie an overhand knot or tailor's knot to secure it.

6. Fold the waistband's seam allowance over and pin. Do the same at the other end of the waistband. Trim seam allowances at the waistline. To avoid a cutting mistake, place one hand between the scissors and the garment while you trim with the other.

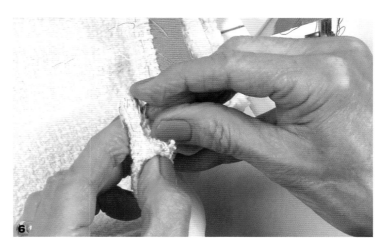

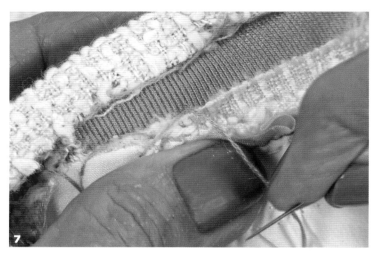

7. Use catchstitches to sew all seam allowances to the waistband. Remove the bastings and press the ends of the waistband firmly.

8. Place a coat hook ⅛ in. from the end of the waistband. Using a double strand of waxed thread, sew the hook eyelets securely with backstitches.

9. Place an eye at the other end of the band so that it is even with the center back edge. Sew securely and then test to make sure the hook and eye are positioned evenly, without a gap. Sew the remaining hook and eye.

LINING THE WAISTBAND

The final step to complete the waistband is to line it. I used the same silk used to line the skirt. In this case, we are using charmeuse silk, although we have opted to use the matte side, which is easier to see for demonstration purposes. Normally, I prefer the shiny side because it feels soft and luxurious against the skin.

1. Cut the lining ¾ in. wider and 1 in. longer than the waistband. Press one long edge under ½ in.

2. With wrong sides together, pin the lining to the waistband, with the folded edge at the top.

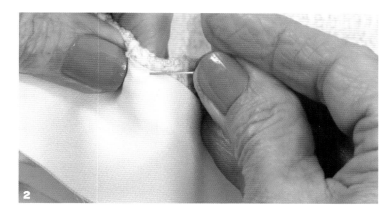

3. Baste the lining in place at the upper edge.

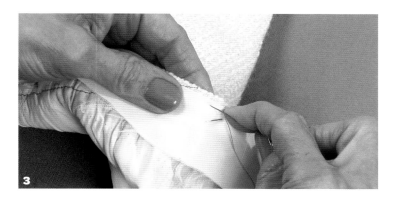

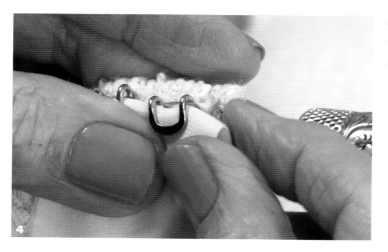

4. Fold the ends under to cover the eyelets on the hooks and eyes. Continue basting.

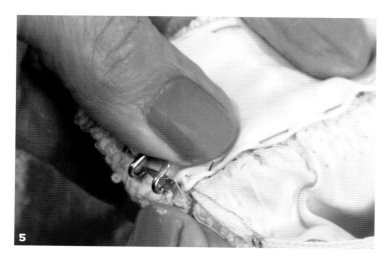

5. When the entire lining has been basted to the waistband, sew it in place permanently using matching thread and slipstitches.

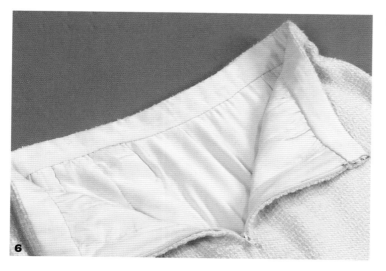

6. Press the finished waistband.

COUTURE COLLECTION

Trimmed with piping, this waistband has been faced with grosgrain. The ribbon may not be original to this 1967 vintage skirt.

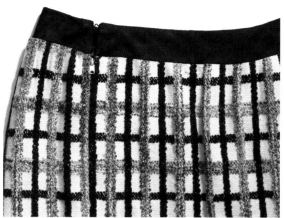

The smallest part of the waist is at the top of this curved navy waistband. The silk shantung of the waistband creates a smooth silhouette in this 1967 skirt.

For the skirt project in this book, we made a self-fabric waistband lined with silk charmeuse and closed it with two coat hooks.

From 1966, this green and black bouclé skirt's waistband is faced.

(Continued on p. 92)

COUTURE COLLECTION (CONTINUED)

The waistband on this Prince of Wales plaid skirt has been enlarged with an inset to the front, hence the unmatched plaids. The skirt was also shortened, so it is possible that a piece of fabric from the hem was used for the alteration.

The edge at the waist in this black skirt is faced, allowing the braid-trimmed edge of the overlap to end at the waistline without interruption.

The shaping on this wide waistband clearly shows the narrowest part of the waist more than halfway below the top edge.

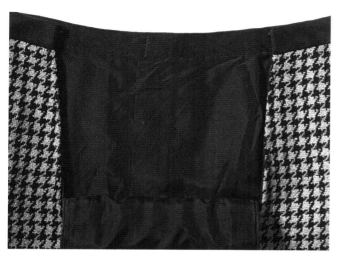

Made from houndstooth silk suiting, this skirt has two seams in the back. Each has a short zipper so it's easier to put on and doesn't show below a jacket.

The silk facing of the waist treatment has been removed to reveal the use of two strips of grosgrain ribbon. The small tucks provide shaping at the narrowest part of the waist, about midway in the wide waistband.

This brown waistband was cut from the fabric selvage edge. The lining extends all the way to the top of the waistband.

CHAPTER EIGHT

The Couture Finish

This wine velvet skirt from the late 1970s is lined with two layers of silk chiffon and fastens with chiffon-covered snaps and a zipper. The waistband is finished with silk satin binding and trimmed with rayon lip braid.

FINISHING DETAILS

In contrast to the simple elegance displayed on the outside of the skirt, the inside reveals solutions to a variety of challenges. For example, loosely woven fabrics are easily stretched out of shape, but the finished skirt hem will remain smooth and flat due to the interfacing. And, many fabrics are bulky—how are the corners finished so smoothly? The answer is a mitered corner. Then there is the matter of the lining. Now that the lining has been quilted to the skirt fabric, how will the edges be finished?

Some of the details shown here may not be visible when the skirt is worn, but they give the wearer the confidence that every aspect of the garment is couture quality, inside and out.

The Chanel Look is designed to flatter women of all ages, from a girl of 19 to a woman of 75.

JOINING THE FAUX WRAP

The front of the skirt features what appears to be a wrap. If we had not removed excess fabric over the stomach area, we could leave this unsewn; however, it would be bulky and not very flattering. Therefore, we will sew it closed using stitches that should be invisible from the front. Let me show you how.

1. Pin the right front to the left at the edge of the overlap for 10 in. Baste about ¼ in. from the edge with a long needle (place a cardboard separator between the front and back of the skirt so you won't catch the skirt back). Use long needles for long stitches such as thread tracing, uneven basting, and stab stitches; use shorter needles for general sewing, short basting stitches, hemming, and other finishing techniques.

2. Using a short needle, sew the overlap permanently. Slipstitches or fell stitches will work, but I prefer blind stitches for a realistic-looking lap.

3. If you have not already done so, sew the seam allowance on the silk and underlap fabric with a catchstitch.

4. Turn the skirt wrong side out. Insert a cardboard separator to make pinning and sewing the underlap easier. Pin the silk edge to the silk lining of the overlap. Baste it in place.

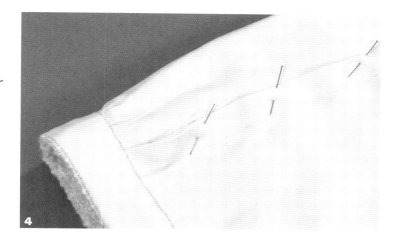

5. Using slipstitches, join the edges permanently.

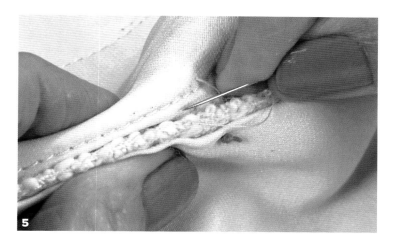

6. Sew a horizontal line of blind stitches connecting the underlap to the overlap. Remove all thread bastings.

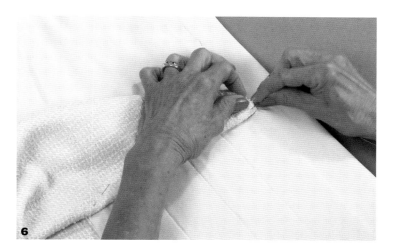

HEMMING

If you have ever made a couture cardigan jacket, you may have sewn a chain along the hem of the jacket to add a little weight and help the jacket hang properly. We won't need that for the couture skirt—a bit of interfacing will suffice to help the skirt hang beautifully and give body to the hem.

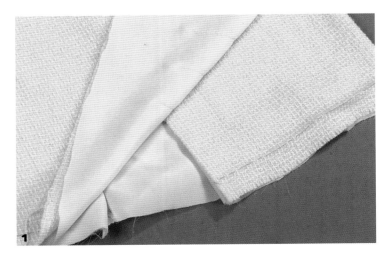

1. The hemline has been marked with basting thread.

2. The hem will be interfaced with a bias-cut strip of silk organza. Fold over ½ in. from the edge and press it.

3. Place the interfacing on the wrong side of the skirt so the folded edge is on the marked hemline. Pin in place.

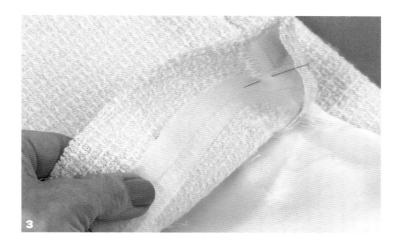

4. Using blind stitches and a long needle, sew the folded edge to the hemline.

5. Fold the hem over the interfacing and baste about ¼ in. from the edge. Start 1 in. from the overlap corner and continue to the underlap corner, stopping 1 in. shy of the end.

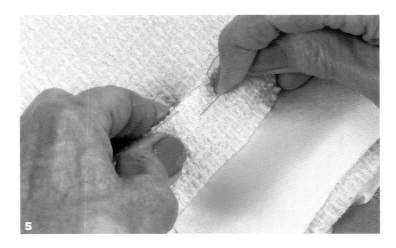

MITERING THE CORNER

1. Clip into the seam allowance of the hem to the corner.

2. Continue to hold the hem with your left thumb. Fold the right side into a miter and pin it.

3. Trim away the excess so the trimmed edges meet.

4. Butt the newly trimmed edges together.

5. Sew the butted edges together.

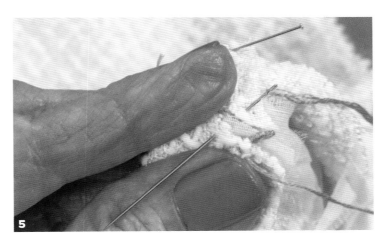

6. Place a pin on the seamline to hold the seam allowance in place. Fold the miter over the hem, and sew the folded edge permanently. Press. Trim the hem allowance to ½ in. Use catch-stitches to sew the hem permanently. Finish the last few inches of the center back seam lining with slip-stitches.

FINISHING THE LINING

We have reached the final step in completing the skirt. The lining hem will now be attached to the skirt fabric. As a final finishing touch, the center front of the skirt is marked with cross-stitches.

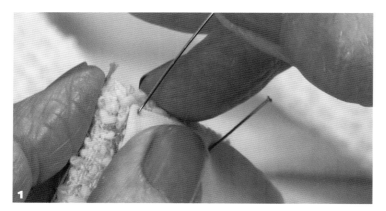

1. Fold under the lining and pin so that it is about ¼ in. from the edge of the hem.

2. Baste the lining to the hem allowance and remove the pins.

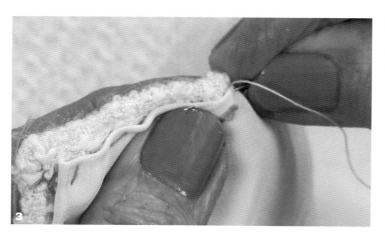

3. Sew the lining to the hem permanently with slipstitches or fell stitches so the stitches do not show on the face of the skirt.

4. On the waistband lining, sew a row of cross-stitches to mark center front.

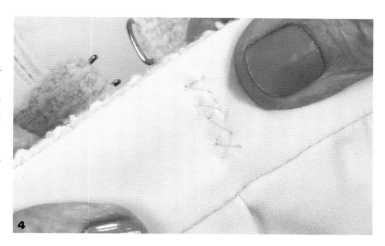

HINT Cross-stitches are made by working two rows of diagonal stitches in opposite directions, one on top of the other. In couture, a large cross-stitch is sometimes used to mark the front, right side, or top of garment sections.

COUTURE COLLECTION

On this skirt, made in 1963, the trim on the overlap is folded over to make the facing on the inside. At the corner, the trim is mitered on the inside and the outside. It is applied like a piping.

CHAPTER NINE

Characteristics of the Chanel Skirt

This Chanel skirt was made in 1967 as part of a jacket and skirt ensemble. It is lined to the edge with navy silk shantung. The quilting lines are spaced rather closely together, every 1⅝ in.

ICONIC DETAILS

Always bold and innovative, Gabrielle (Coco) Chanel introduced her cardigan skirt suit almost a hundred years ago. Today it is more popular than ever. Why? What is it about this outfit that has made it the single most important and most copied design in fashion history? Softly tailored, the skirts are simply styled, using the same lightweight fabrics as the jackets, and, when first introduced, they were an extraordinary contrast to the full skirts and multiple petticoats that they replaced. It's easy to see why they became instant favorites.

Deceptively simple in appearance, the skirts are gracefully engineered to flatter the figure and move with the body. Practical, yet elegant without obvious effort, the skirts feature luxury fabrics, simplicity of design, and attention to detail, and they function to empower women and provide them with the confidence that the design is equally perfect for a society maven, business executive, or busy mom. Through the years, the skirts have encompassed a variety of designs, such as the simple A-line, flares, pleats, and the straight skirt with a faux wrap described in this book. All are comfortable to wear, facilitate easy movement, and flatter several figure types—important elements for success.

WHAT'S SO SPECIAL ABOUT CHANEL SKIRTS?

Chanel skirts appear to be basic, uncomplicated garments, but in reality, they're very complex. Nothing is left to chance in either the construction or the fit. Every detail is part of a master plan to control the garment's drape, prolong its pristine appearance, and enhance the wearer even after repeated wearing. The techniques used to accomplish these things—the shaping, quilting, and finishing—are labor intensive.

Chanel's skirts are inconspicuously shaped to gently follow the curves of the body. The fabric is manipulated so seams are replaced by darts and darts are replaced by ease or shorter darts. The simplicity of the basic design is the primary reason it can be modified and reinvented by changing the fabric, trims, buttons, and other design features.

LUXURIOUS FABRICS AND TRIMS

Chanel shocked the fashion world when, early in her career, she began making suits from soft jersey knits she had purchased in quantity from the textile manufacturer Jean Rodier. Not one to follow the rules, Chanel again made headlines when she began using menswear plaids and tweeds for women's suits. Over the years, this timeless suit has most often been made from luxurious wool bouclés and tweeds, but there are many versions in checks, plaids, houndstooths, denim, and stripes. Follow Chanel's lead and think outside the box when making a fabric selection—the jacket can be made in almost any fabric and for any occasion, from sporty to evening. You are limited only by your imagination.

Unlike the jackets, many skirts have no trim, while others feature the same trim as the jacket.

INNOVATIVE CONSTRUCTION TECHNIQUES

Haute couture construction techniques require a lot of hand sewing, and this skirt is no exception. Couture workrooms use hand sewing because it affords greater control—easing and shaping can be introduced easily during the assembly process. Stretching and shrinking are methods that many couture houses, including Chanel, frequently use to engineer both the fit and the design of the garment. Chanel is also credited with introducing quilting to high-fashion garments. We can only guess the reasons. In the late teens, there was a shortage of heavier fabrics, and quilting was used

This is the pink bouclé skirt sewn for this book. I chose not to apply any trim because I will wear it with different jackets, each of which has been finished with different trims and embellishments.

to provide warmth. During the Comeback years, the reason for the quilting could have been to stabilize and add body to the soft, lightweight fabrics that tended to droop or stretch out of shape easily, or to maintain the shaping that had been added with heat and moisture. By quilting the fabric to the delicate lining fabric, without any filler material, the skirts have structure without stiffness so they maintain the design and desired comfort level.

The side seams are generally eliminated, and the curved section of the seam from waist to hip is replaced with darts. When the fabric permits, the darts are converted to ease and shrunk until they fit smoothly. When darts are used, they're small and short and positioned to flatter the figure.

This straight skirt from 1960 has two zippers in the back and a center front seam. There are no traditional side seams at all. The silk waistband folds over at the waistline, much like a binding.

DISTINCTIVE DESIGN DETAILS

One of Chanel's most famous styles—the wrap skirt—rarely, if ever, wraps. It's just an illusion; it is a traditional skirt with a thigh-high slit and a fake wrap with a zipper or zippers on the skirt back. My skirt has a single seam at center back, but many Chanel skirts have two seams on the side backs. Having two zippers facilitates dressing and prevents the zippers from showing below the jacket hem.

Generally, the wrap is on the skirt front, but it can be on the back or on both the front and back. Most skirts wrap right over left, but a few wrap left over right.

The shaping on this skirt was done so skillfully that the plaid itself seems to change shape on the side of the skirt, between the waist and hips. Notice how the white squares get smaller, but the navy bars remain consistently sized. Small darts were taken out of the white fabric.

COPIES AND KNOCKOFFS

When Chanel opened her boutique in Deauville in 1913, American publications had been reporting on French fashions for more than a century, and it was not unusual for American manufacturers and dressmakers to copy Parisian designs for their clients in the early years of the 20th century. The simplicity of the Chanel designs was perfect for inspiration and adaptations. Some were copied precisely using the same fabrics and design features as the originals, while others were adapted so they could be manufactured less expensively. It has been reported that Chanel loved to see copies of her clothes running about the streets, and considered that the only way to measure a designer's success. In fact, Chanel felt it was so important to be copied that she contacted American manufacturers before she showed her Comeback Collection in 1954 to give them the opportunity to see it and begin planning their knockoffs. Being a savvy businesswoman, Chanel charged buyers and manufacturers a fee to see the advanced collection. This fee is called a "caution," and it could be as much as $3,200—a great deal of money in 1957.

The caution at most couture houses allowed the buyer to choose two designs for copying. Then he or she would be given Chanel's *Fiche de Références*—a one-page list of resources—for each design and granted the rights to make and sell authentic, licensed copies. The reference list included a sketch of the design and a description of the fabrics, the manufacturer, color, style number, and precisely how much was needed for each garment as well as similar details for the trims and buttons.

The most expensive copies were line-for-line designs, or *répétitions*, custom-made for a specific client in the couture workrooms at stores such as I. Magnin in San Francisco, Julius Garfinkel in Washington, D.C., and Bergdorf Goodman and Chez Ninon in New York, who made suits for Jacqueline Kennedy when she was First Lady. After the client placed her order, the head of the workroom would order the same materials used by Chanel from Linton Tweeds, Bianchini, Abraham, or Chantal for her. Then a pattern would be made on the client's dress form, and the garment would be custom-made by American needleworkers who had the same skills as their counterparts in the Chanel ateliers so the workmanship and quality of the répétitions were as good as the original Chanels. Several years ago, I compared a Dior original and a copy made in the I. Magnin workroom. The techniques were slightly different, but the quality was comparable. Sometimes they even cost as much, but the client enjoyed the convenience of being fitted at a local retailer and not having to spend a month in Paris.

READY-TO-WEAR LICENSED COPIES

American manufacturers used a variety of industry techniques to modify the pattern inconspicuously for the mass production of ready-to-wear garments. Even though they used the same fabrics, trims, and buttons as Chanel, their labor costs were much lower, so they could sell them for about one-tenth the price of an original Chanel. Davidow was the most important of these manufacturers; others included Jablow, Harry Frechtel, Seymour Fox, Nan Herzlinger, Burke-Amey, Anne Rubin, Andrew Arkin, Molly for Jack Sarnoff, Vera Stewart, and Saks Fifth Ave. In England, the Wallis shops purchased several designs each season to copy for their customers. When a Chanel original was shown in the editorial pages of *Vogue*, these manufacturers were mentioned. The photo caption would include the manufacturer's name and a list of stores where the copies were sold as well as stores that sold the Chanel original. This made Chanel styles available at several price points. Sadly, few museums collect authorized copies of Chanel designs, and only one—the Fashion Institute of Technology in New York—has a copy and an original of the same model.

This copy by Davidow has no side seams and a dart at the side, as opposed to easing. The lining is probably a rayon shantung, and it is not quilted.

AMERICAN CHANELS

Almost immediately, the manufacturers who made licensed copies—as well as designers such as Larry Aldrich, Lilli Ann, Burke-Amey, and Traina-Norell—began creating their own "American Chanels." Some of these designs were made from the same fabrics as Chanel, while others were not. The most identifiable differences of these adaptations were the buttons, since they did not feature a Chanel logo. In more recent years, collections of knit suits by Adolfo, St. John Knits, and Castleberry have been inspired by Chanel's cardigan suits.

COMPARISON OF COUTURE CHANEL SKIRT AND DAVIDOW COPY

From 1964, the left skirt on the facing page is fabricated in a wool and mohair fabric from Linton Tweeds. The fabric was woven in a plaid pattern, then piece-dyed to create subtle variations in the color. The faux-wrap skirt has four gores; the side seams were replaced with easing and short darts. The skirt was shaped to fit a client with a high left hip. The fabric was trimmed on the underlap to reduce bulk over the stomach.

The skirt is lined to the edges with a lightweight plain-weave silk and vertically quilted at 1¼-in. intervals. The lining is finished with slipstitches at the edges of the faux wrap and hem.

The edge of the faux wrap and the hem are trimmed with a 1¼-in-wide decorative band that has been embroidered vertically with yarns that match the skirt, then embroidered horizontally with additional matching yarns and metallic threads. The overlap was sewn to the underlap with blindstitches placed about 1 in. from the edge.

Only ¾ in. wide, the waistband is trimmed with selvage and faced with petersham ribbon. A row of cross-stitches marks the center front on the petersham. At the zipper placket, the band has a small point on the overlap and fastens with a single coat hook and eye. Placed on the left hip, the zipper is not original.

From 1967, the attractive Davidow skirt on the right side on the facing page is part of a three-piece ensemble—jacket, skirt, and blouse—licensed by Chanel. The suit is well made and would have cost about one-tenth as much as the original couture suit. Licensed copies are no longer available since Chanel markets its own ready-to-wear in boutiques around the world. The unquilted skirt is fabricated in a high-quality wool plaid that is beautifully matched horizontally. The four-gored skirt has a faux wrap with long darts replacing the side seams. The right front—the overlap—is sewed into the seam on the left front by machine.

The vertical match is less perfect where the dark green color bars are extra wide at some seams. The excess wool has been trimmed away on the underlap to reduce bulk over the stomach.

The wool is used for the one-piece waistband and wraps the edge to face the band. The 1-in.-wide waistband has a ½-in. overlap and a 2-in. underlap so it can be adjusted at the waist. The band fastens with two hooks and eyes.

Made of lightweight rayon shantung, the skirt lining is open at the hem and finished with a 3-in.-wide machine-stitched hem. Hand-sewn with blind stitches, the skirt hem is also 3 in. wide and finished with monofilament thread serging. The seams are pinked on the lining with no finish on the skirt seams. The center front is identified on a cloth label on the waistband facing.

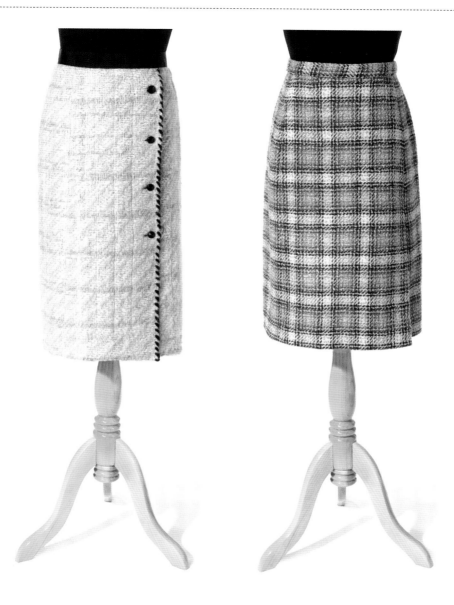

DAVIDOW, INC.

Davidow was the most famous manufacturer of licensed Chanel copies. The Special Collections at the Fashion Institute of Technology in New York City has the Davidow Archives with the Fiche de Rèferences for many of the Davidow copies, including a Chanel sketch for the design, sometimes fabric swatches, and a list of all fabrics, linings, notions, buttons, and trims used to make it. The fabrics are described in detail: manufacturer, style number, color, and exact yardage amount for the design.

CHRONOLOGY OF COCO CHANEL AND THE HOUSE OF CHANEL

According to Chanel, "My life didn't please me, so I created my life." Consequently, research into the early years finds many discrepancies of dates and mysteries of authenticity. In an effort to get to the truth, I relied first on publications of the period such as *Women's Wear Daily*, *Vogue* (American and British), *Harper's Bazaar*, and *Elle*, then on fashion historians Amy de la Haye and Valerie Steele, and lastly on the biographers who knew her. There is no question that Chanel was very successful, but it's quite possible that she popularized many designs instead of inventing them. We may never know the true details of her career, and since she outlived her competitors, there was no one to contradict her claims.

1883	August 19, born Gabrielle Bonheur Chanel.	
1908	Begins a hat-making career in Paris at 160 boulevard Malesherbes.	
1910	Opens a millinery shop, Chanel Modes, in Paris at 21 rue Cambon.	
1913	Opens a boutique in Deauville.	
	Introduces the unlined sport coat, made in Rodier jersey.	
1914	Introduces jersey sweaters that slip on over the head.	
	Introduces the two-piece swimsuit.	
1915	Opens her first couture house in Biarritz on the Côte Basque.	
	A Chanel dress costs 3,000 French francs (approximately $600 in 1915).	
1916	Introduces the sport outfit: a coat and dress or coat and skirt.	
	First published sketch of a Chanel chemise design appears in *Harper's Bazaar*.	
	Chanel knockoffs sold in New York at Leo D. Greenfield, Inc.	
1917	Introduces the jersey jacket, lined with fabric to match dress.	
	Jacket trimmed (and possibly lined) with plaid to match skirt.	
1919	Opens her couture house at 31 rue Cambon, which is still in operation today.	
	Registers as a *couturière* (dressmaker).	
1920	Introduces the quilted coat.	
1921	Introduces the collarless, boxy cardigan jacket with skirt.	
	Launches Chanel No. 5 perfume, developed by perfume house of Rallet, sold exclusively in her boutiques.	
	Commissions embroidery from House of Kitmir.	
	Establishes the iconic double C logo.	
1922	Designs costumes for the play *Antigone* written by Jean Cocteau.	
1923	Opens a boutique in Cannes.	
	Makes the short chemise invented by Paul Poiret famous.	
1924	Establishes Société Parfums Chanel with Pierre and Paul Wertheimer and Théophile Bader to produce and market Chanel No. 5 and the first line of makeup, featuring lip colors and face powders.	
1925	Introduces the jersey Chanel suit.	
1926	Introduces a Little Black Dress that *Vogue* called the "Chanel Ford."	
	Chanel models are copied in all prices from $10 to $250.	

1926	Employs 2,000 workers and produces 20,000 originals a year.	
1927	Opens a couture house in London; closes Biarritz.	
	Duke of Westminster puts CC logo on lamppost in Mayfair (London).	
1928	Opens Tricot Chanel textiles; incorporates tweeds (traditional menswear fabrics) into her line.	
	Best & Co. (New York) advertises "Chanel" coats—copies of the popular Chanel chamois coat.	
1929	Introduces the unisex style.	
	Opens Boutique on rue Cambon to sell perfume.	
1930	Introduces braid trims in her designs.	
1931	Goes to Hollywood to design costumes for MGM.	
1933	Renames Tricot Chanel to Tissus Chanel.	
1935	At the peak of her career, employs 4,000 workers, owns five boutiques on rue Cambon, and sells 28,000 suits a year worldwide.	
1936	Employees strike and lock Chanel out.	
1939	Closes her couture house when France declares war on Germany.	
1940	Moves to the Ritz for the duration of World War II.	
1946	Moves to Switzerland and lives in self-imposed exile.	
1953	Returns to Paris and reopens her couture house with 350 employees.	
1954	Shows first collection of the Comeback years.	
	Sells Chanel Couture to Pierre Wertheimer and Les Parfums Chanel, May 24.	
1955	Creates classic quilted bag with chain named "2.55" for its debut date, February 1955.	
1956	Hires Jean Cazaubon and Yvonne Dudel as design assistants.	
	Reintroduces the braid-trimmed Chanel suit.	
1957	Receives the Neiman Marcus Fashion Award for Distinguished Service in the Field of Fashion.	
	Creates the legendary two-tone, slingback shoe.	
	"Chanel look" described as a style by the *New York Times*.	
	"Chaneleries" used by *Elle* magazine, October 28.	
1958	*Vogue* magazine coins the term "Chanelisms," September 1.	
1960	Chanel couture suit costs about $1,000.	

	"Chanel marrow" used by *Harper's Bazaar*, March.	
1963	Jacqueline Kennedy wears a Chanel *répétition* made by Chez Ninon (New York) to Dallas.	
	London Sunday Times proposes naming Chanel "First Fashion Immortal."	
1969	Davidow copies of Chanel suits cost about $350.	
1971	January 10, Coco Chanel dies at the Ritz in Paris.	
	Gaston Berthelot hired to oversee production of Chanel designs.	
1973	Ramon Esparza replaces Berthelot to design couture.	
1973	Jean Cazaubon and Yvonne Dudel take over couture designs at Chanel.	
1973	Davidow, Inc., an American manufacturer known for its Chanel copies, closes.	
1974	Alain Wertheimer (Pierre's grandson) becomes CEO; refuses licensing deals.	
1978	Establishment of Chanel Creations, the first Chanel ready-to-wear line, designed by Philippe Guibourgé.	
	Chanel Creations cost about $750; haute couture designs cost about $4,000.	
1983	Karl Lagerfeld appointed Artistic Director of Chanel Fashion, designer of all haute couture, ready-to-wear, and accessory collections, a position he holds today.	
	Chanel couture suits cost $6,000 to $15,000+; ready-to-wear suits cost $3,000.	
1997	Acquires Maison Lemarié (feathers).	
2002	Acquires Lesage (embroidery), Maison Michel (millinery), Massaro (shoemaking), and Desrues (ornamentation and costume jewelry).	
2002	Establishes Paraffection to include all specialty ateliers to preserve the unique expertise of fashion's traditional craftsmen.	
2005	Acquires Robert Goossens (gold- and silversmithing) and Massaro (bootmaking).	
	The Metropolitan Museum of Art in New York honors Chanel with a grand exhibition dedicated to the House of Chanel.	
2006	Acquires Guillet (fabric flowers).	
2011	Acquires Montex (embroidery).	
2012	Chanel Paraffection purchases Barrie Knitwear in Hawick, Scotland.	
2013	Chanel haute couture suit costs approximately $50,000; ready-to-wear jacket costs $6,000 to $12,000.	

WHEN WAS IT MADE?

My collection encompasses Chanel's Comeback years (1954–1971), what I call the In-Between years (1971–1983), and the Lagerfeld years (1983–present). Dating vintage garments can be a challenge, especially when purchased from secondhand stores or online auctions. As a collector, I've spent nearly as much time dating the more than 100 Chanel originals and copies I own, as I have examining their structure and design. Here are some of my discoveries.

Most Chanel suits have a label only on the jacket. Under the label there is a tape—the bolduc—with a number on it. These are reference numbers for the Chanel archives. In addition to the date purchased, the archive records would include the name of the client; the cost of the suit; details about the fabrics, trims, and notions used to make the suit as well as the workroom(s) where it was made; and the number of hours required to make it. With this in mind, I record the number of every garment I examine. Sadly, some have no labels, and on others, the number has faded and cannot be read. Without access to the Chanel archives—which are not open to the public—I found other ways to date the garments. I looked through old issues of *Vogue*, *Harper's Bazaar*, and *Elle* for photographs of suits. I was first able to precisely date one photographed by *Vogue* in 1960, and so the list began. The earliest suit I have was pictured on the cover of *Elle* in 1957. Slowly my list came together and is shown here.

YEAR	BOLDUC NUMBER
• 1957	05600–05900
• 1960	12000–15200
• 1962	17000
• 1964	23000–24000
• 1965	26000–28000
• 1966	31500
• 1967	33500–34000
• 1969	36000–39687
• 1970	38981
• 1971	41500–43000
• 1972	44000
• 1973	47500
• 1975	53000
• 1983	63750
• 1989	68000
• 1991	69750
• 1992	70000
• 1993	71500
• 1995	73200
• 2003	81500

TECHNIQUES FOR WAISTBANDS

Only three techniques are used extensively in couture for finishing the waist edges of skirts: the self-fabric band, the faced band, and the faced edge, which does not have a band. Appropriate for lined or unlined skirts, the faced waistband is finished with a lining fabric facing or grosgrain ribbon applied by hand. This versatile method is suitable for a variety of waistband designs, fabrics, and figures.

PREPARE THE WAISTBAND

Sewn from the same fabric as the skirt, the waistband can be cut on the lengthwise grain or crossgrain if the fabric pattern is being matched. It's rarely cut on the more easily shaped bias, except when it matches the blouse fabric and a bias cut is unnoticeable. Most finished bands are 1 in. to $1^1/4$ in. wide. They can fasten with lapped or abutted ends. Use these directions for self-fabric and faced bands.

1. To determine the finished length of the band, measure your waist and add 2-in. ease.

HINT   I use a muslin strip instead of a tape measure, pin it around my waist, and sit down to be sure it's comfortable. Then I measure the strip.

2. Thread-trace the band's finished length and desired width on a large fabric scrap, leaving at least a $1/2$-in. seam allowance on all sides and 3 in. extra length, if you plan to lap the ends.

   Thread-trace all matchpoints and guidelines at garment centers, side seams, and the foldline for a self-fabric waistband. When planning a lap on the skirt back, I place the underlap on the right back.

3. Cut the interfacing the width and length of the finished band. If the fabric is medium to heavy weight, choose a crisp interfacing material like hair canvas, tailor's linen, petersham, woven belting, or grosgrain ribbon. For lightweight fabrics, select woven belting or grosgrain ribbon. If the band is wide or shaped, the interfacing should be crisper than for a straight, narrow band. If one layer of interfacing isn't crisp enough, use two or more layers. With wrong side up, baste the interfacing to the band.

HINT   I use hair canvas scraps and quilt two layers together using zigzag stitches with rows spaced about $1/4$ in. apart.

SELF-FABRIC BAND

Sometimes called a regular or one-piece waistband, the self-fabric band is used on light- and medium-weight fabrics.

1. Apply the interfacing to the thread-traced band by catchstitching the edges of the interfacing to the band.

2. With wrong sides together, fold the waistband on the foldline. Use steam to shape the band for a smoother fit, and stretch the upper edge so it's long enough to fit smoothly around the rib cage. To create a longer line for a short-waisted figure, stretch the bottom of the band so the top edge is at the waistline.

3. With right sides together, align the matchpoints on the band and skirt; baste. Machine-stitch and trim the seam to $1/2$ in.

4. Remove the bastings and press the seam toward the band.

SELF-FABRIC BAND

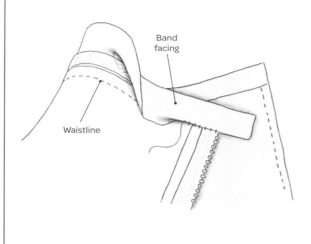

Band facing

Waistline

5. With right sides together, fold the band on the foldline, and baste the ends without catching the skirt. Stitch.

6. Press the seams open, trim, and turn the band right side out.

7. To finish the band, turn under the raw edge like a blouse cuff and fell-stitch the folded edge to the seamline.

FACED WAISTBAND

The faced waistband is smoother and thinner than the self-fabric waistband. It is shaped and sewn almost completely by hand. This is the waistband I used for my skirt.

1. Using the directions on the facing page, apply the interfacing to the thread-traced band. When sewing on wool and hair fibers, press to marry the fibers of the interfacing and fabric.

2. Wrap and pin the seam allowances around the interfacing and baste them in place for the fitting. Don't worry about the bulk at the corners.

3. Use steam to shape the band for a smoother fit, stretching the upper edge so it's long enough to fit smoothly around the rib cage.

4. Baste the band to the skirt for the fitting. If the band rolls, the interfacing is not crisp enough, the band is too tight, or the fabric is unusually bulky. Lengthen the band so it's comfortable, using some of the 3-in. lap.

5. After the fitting, mark any corrections with contrasting thread. Remove the band.

6. Release the bastings holding the seam allowances in place at the ends and lower edge. Remove just enough of the bastings at the top of the band to release the ends. Trim the interfacing so it extends only 2 in. beyond the opening and does not extend into the end seam allowances.

7. With right sides together, baste the lower edge of the band to the skirt, aligning the seamlines and matchpoints; stitch. Remove the basting and press the seam flat, then open and press the waist seam toward the band.

HINT When the fabric is bulky, I clip the skirt seam allowance about 1 in. from the end of the band.

---

8. Grade the skirt seam allowance so the raw edge is about $1/8$ in. below the raw edge of the band seam allowance.

9. On most light- and medium-weight fabrics, the corners of the band can be finished neatly without mitering. Baste next to the interfacing at the ends. Taper the end seam allowances so they won't show when the ends are folded under. Trim away a small triangle at the end of the interfacing. Trim at the center so they don't overlap; press.

FINISHING ENDS
OF BAND

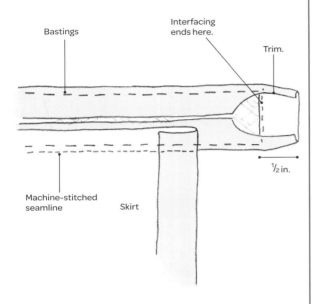

Bastings

Interfacing ends here.

Trim.

Machine-stitched seamline

Skirt

½ in.

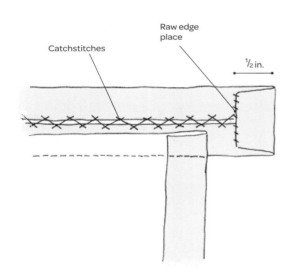

Catchstitches

Raw edge place

½ in.

10. Fold under the ends of the band, baste them in place, and press again. Spank the ends briskly with a clapper to flatten them. Trim away any stray threads, and sew the ends securely with small whipstitches or catchstitches. Use catchstitches to sew the fabric to the interfacing.

When the fabric is bulky, miter all corners except the bottom corner on the overlap (see p. 102 for mitering corners).

11. Topstitch the band ¼ in. from the edges and waistline seam, if desired.

12. If the design has belt loops, fold the loops to the wrong side of the band so each has ⅛ in. to ⅜ in. of play; sew each loop permanently by hand.

COMPLETE AND FACE THE BAND

Before completing the band, add the lining and hanger loops, if any, as well as the hooks and eyes on the band.

1. If the skirt will be lined, assemble the lining and place it inside the skirt with wrong sides together, matching the seamlines at the waist and aligning the seams and darts; pin. Use short running stitches to sew the skirt and lining together about ⅛ in. above the waistband seam.

2. Use large hooks and eyes to fasten the skirt. To attach the hooks on the overlap, begin with the wrong side up. Sew two hooks so the ends of the hooks are set back ⅛ in. from the end of the band.

3. With right side up, use blanket stitches to sew the corresponding straight eyes on the underlap. If the band ends abut, sew two round eyes to the wrong side of the underlap so the ends meet. Continuing on the underlap, sew a round eye at the end. Sew the corresponding hook securely on the underside of the overlap so the band will fit snugly.

4. Before setting the facing, attach hanger loops to the skirt so they lap the seamline by ⅜ in.

5. Cut the band facing on the lengthwise grain from lining fabric so it is $\frac{1}{4}$ in. longer and wider than the finished band. Grosgrain ribbon is an optional facing, and the long edges are already finished. Cut it $\frac{3}{4}$ in. longer.

6. With wrong sides together, center the facing over the band. Use an awl to make a hole in the facing for the hook sewn farthest from the end of the band. Push the threads aside and slip the hook through the facing. Pin the facing and band together.

7. Turn under the edges of the facing at the top and ends so the facing is about $\frac{1}{8}$ in. from the band edges; pin. At the end of the overlap, tuck the folded edge under the hooks; pin. At the waist, turn under the raw edge so it barely covers the running stitches; pin. Baste and press lightly. Fell-stitch the facing to the band, remove the bastings, and press. For a grosgrain facing, turn under the ends. Baste all edges and fell-stitch them permanently.

FACED WAISTLINE

Usually finished with a grosgrain ribbon facing, or lining, the faced waistline was favored by Chanel for many skirts. Since it doesn't include a waistband, this finish is often used on skirts that accompany overblouses. The facing is applied by hand and can be designed so either the bottom or top of the interfacing sits at the waistline. These directions are for a grosgrain ribbon facing.

1. Fit the skirt with a stay tape at the waist and interface the top of the skirt as needed.

2. Fold under the skirt seam allowance to enclose the stay tape. Use catchstitches to sew the seam allowance to the interfacing.

3. Shape the grosgrain to fit the curve of the waist using a steam iron, small darts, or small snips at the bottom of the ribbon. When using snips, overcast the edges to prevent raveling.

4. With wrong side up, place the grosgrain on the skirt just below the waist edge. Fell-stitch the edges in place. Turn under the ends and baste.

ADDING FACING TO WAISTBAND

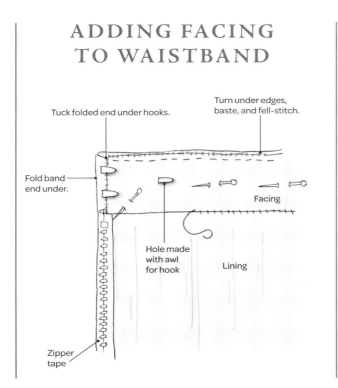

Tuck folded end under hooks.

Turn under edges, baste, and fell-stitch.

Fold band end under.

Facing

Hole made with awl for hook

Lining

Zipper tape

FACED WAISTLINE

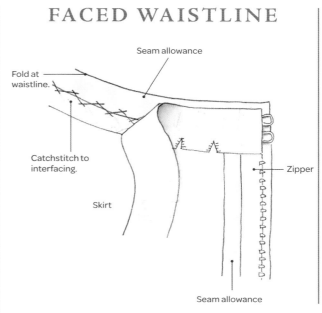

Seam allowance

Fold at waistline.

Catchstitch to interfacing.

Skirt

Zipper

Seam allowance

JOINING A SKIRT TO A FOUNDATION

Some skirts are joined to foundations—a full slip or camisole—and are more comfortable to wear, but the hang of the garment is affected.

Skirts can be sewn to a blouse, slip, or camisole, or to a waist cincher. These skirts are usually designed to be worn with a separate, but specific, overblouse or tunic, and become a two-piece dress.

Alternatively, the skirt can be first joined to the foundation and then the bodice sewn to the foundation. When complete, the garment is a dress, but it begins with a skirt-foundation construction. This technique is one way to create a blouson bodice, but it's equally effective for a fitted bodice.

1. Fit the foundation and stitch permanently.

2. Thread-trace a seamline on the foundation where you plan to set the skirt. It can be parallel to the floor, follow the contour of the waist, or be completely different. To reduce bulk at the waistline, the skirt can be set several inches below the natural waistline.

3. Joining the skirt is much easier if you have a dress form. Put the foundation on it; pin the skirt to it, aligning any thread tracings and matchpoints. If you don't have a form, ask a friend to pin it in place when you try it on.

Depending on the desired effect, the skirt seam allowance can be pressed with the raw edge pointing toward the shoulders to produce a flatter seam, or it can be turned under with a buttressed seam so that the top of the skirt will stand away from the body; this is especially appropriate for bouffant petticoats and evening skirts.

4. Check the hang of the skirt; correct as needed.

5. Remove the foundation and skirt. Baste them together, and examine the results.

6. If the skirt hangs properly, sew it in place permanently. For a flat finish, trim the skirt seam allowance to $^1/_4$ in. to $^3/_8$ in. wide; use catchstitches to neaten the trimmed edge or cover it with seam binding. For a buttressed seam, slipstitch the skirt to the foundation and overcast the raw edge.

7. To attach a bodice to the foundation, put the foundation and skirt back on the dress form or fit them again on the figure. Pin the bodice in place, aligning any matchpoints and adjusting the length as desired for a smoothly fitted torso or for a blouson effect. Finish the waistline of the bodice by folding the raw edge under or covering it with a band of matching or contrasting fabric. Sew the attaching seam by hand.

1

2

GARMENT INDEX

The garments featured in this book are from my own vintage collection, which has grown to more than 2,000 couture and high-end ready-to-wear designs since I began collecting in the 1970s. They are all Chanel originals from the 1960s, 1970s, and 1980s, except for the Davidow authorized copy and three skirts that I made. All were selected because they allow the wearer to move easily. Some have the faux wrap, which is covered in this book; others have flares, pleats, or vents.

WOOL PLAID

1. This skirt from the late 1960s has knife pleats with a wide box pleat at center front. The pleats begin just below the hips. When the pleats open up, you can see that the original fabric pattern has a narrow navy stripe, but the top of the skirt has been seamed to make a wider stripe above the pleats. The underlays of the pleats have been trimmed away; to keep them from sagging, a silk stay was joined to the waistline and top of the pleats. This skirt has no hem. It had been shortened by another owner, so it distorted the skirt's proportion. The skirt has a single zipper on the left hip. The skirt has no label or number; the bolduc number on the jacket is 33214.

WOOL TWEED

2. Made of wool and mohair tweed from Linton Tweed, this skirt has a faux wrap. The piping and facing on the overlap and hem edges were cut from the wrong side of an aqua stripe on the blouse fabric. The skirt is quilted at the edges of the narrow cream stripes and the waistband is faced with grosgrain. The overlap is sewn to the underlap by hand for $12^1/2$ in. The skirt has four gores with a lap zipper on the left hip and no side seams. It has no label; the bolduc number on the jacket is 33418.

3

4

SILK FAILLE

3. Fabricated in cream-colored silk, this stunning skirt was photographed for the March 1, 1963, issue of *Vogue* magazine. The skirt is lined with a plain-weave silk and is not quilted. The unlined overskirt on the front wraps around to the back. The trim on the edges of the overskirt is a flat ¹/2-in.-wide self-fabric piping. At the corners, the trim is mitered on both the face side and the wrong side. The narrow silk waistband is a bias binding. The skirt has no label; the bolduc number on the jacket is 19629.

WOOL CHENILLE PLAID

4. Fabricated in a plaid from Linton Tweeds, this suit was photographed for the March 1, 1965, issue of *Vogue*. The skirt has hand-painted buttons, handmade thread buttonholes, and a chenille yarn trim at the edge. The quilting rows are spaced 1³/4 in. apart. At the waist, the skirt was first sewn to two rows of petersham to give it shape, then covered with a double layer of 3-in.-wide bias-cut silk, which would have matched the blouse fabric. The upper row of petersham was shaped with steam and heat while the second row was shaped with small darts. A facing would have been applied to the inside to cover the petersham. This was the first Chanel suit I bought. The skirt, like many, had been badly altered and shortened. The skirt has no label; the bolduc number on the suit is 27557.

5

6

7

DAVIDOW COPY

5. Davidow was known for its high-quality Chanel copies; this skirt is a copy of a design in the 1967 collection and would have cost about one-tenth as much as the original suit. The four-gored skirt has no side seams, and it is not quilted to the non-silk lining. Instead of easing at the waist, the shaping was achieved with darts at the sides. The waistband is finished with self-fabric on the inside and has an underlap at the opening. There is a tag at center front.

WOOL PLAID

6. This skirt from the late 1960s has a wide faux wrap that extends almost to the sides. Lined to the edge with a lightweight silk, the quilting rows are spaced 1 3/4 in. apart. The edges are trimmed with self-fabric selvage and embroidered with gold threads and pink yarns. The skirt has four gores and no side seams; the zipper is on the left hip. The selvage edge of the fabric was used to make the waistband with a grosgrain

ribbon facing. The center front is marked with cross-stitches on the grosgrain. There is no label on the skirt; the bolduc number on the jacket is 35228.

WOOL DRESS

7. Although you may be surprised to see a dress in a book about skirts, the construction of this dress is not unusual for couture designs. The technique ensures that the blouse stays in the desired position when the ensemble is worn, and when the bodice opens at center front, the skirt opening is often shifted to the side front to avoid bunching when the wearer sits. The skirt was assembled first with a grosgrain ribbon waistband, and then the bodice was sewn to the waistband, which becomes the waist stay on the finished dress. Tucks on the inside of the skirt at the top are used to create an attractive flare. To maintain the shape, a cotton backing was applied to the center back panel. The dress has no label; the bolduc number on the jacket is 40350.

8

9

SILK HOUNDSTOOTH SUITING

8. Fabricated in a silk suiting with a houndstooth pattern, this skirt was photographed in the March 16, 1960, issue of *Vogue* magazine. The skirt has a center front seam and two seams at the side back to facilitate dressing. There are no side seams. The silk lining is open at the hem; it is not quilted. A lightweight silk backing was applied to the center back panel after the seams were stitched. The serged edge on the hem is not original. Cross-stitches mark the center front on the inside of the waistband. There is no label; the bolduc number on the jacket is 11992.

SILK TWEED

9. Designed for an article in *Threads* magazine, this timeless design features the faux wrap. The skirt fabric is a silk suiting with a microfiber lining, which was selected to match a blouse. There are no side seams, and all darts were replaced by easing. The quilting rows are spaced 2 in. apart. Fabricated in the blouse/lining fabric, the waistband binds the edge. At the center back opening, the waistband abuts and is fastened with coat hooks and eyes. Cross-stitches on the inside of the waistband mark the center front. Like the Chanel designs, the skirt fabric is trimmed away at the top of the underlap.

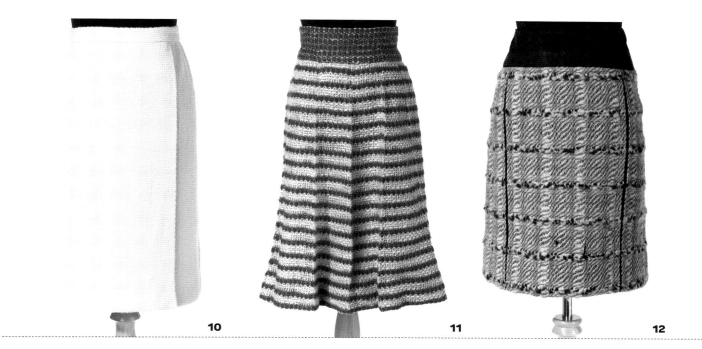

10

11

12

NOVELTY WEAVE RAYON

10. Fabricated in a novelty-weave cotton/rayon, the material was selected because of its color so you could easily see the basting threads during construction and the seams when stitched. The faux wrap design began with a simple straight skirt. The side seams were converted to darts, then all darts were replaced with easing. The skirt has a single seam at center back with the faux wrap in front. It is quilted to silk charmeuse at 2-in. intervals to preserve the shape and add body. At the top of the zipper, there is a "pocket" to hide the zipper tab. The waistband is finished with a silk facing. It is not trimmed since it will be worn with two different jackets.

OPEN-WEAVE STRIPE

11. Fabricated in a novelty open-weave stripe and underlined with beige silk, this flared skirt from the late 1960s has seven gores. At each seam, the edges are topstitched on the outside to simulate pleats. To create the solid color waistband, the beige stripes were removed by tucking. The finished 3$\frac{1}{2}$-in. band required 7$\frac{1}{2}$ in. of untucked fabric. The waistband is faced with lightweight plain-weave silk lining and fastened with seven coat hooks and eyes. Unquilted, the skirt's lining is sewn to the hem. The zipper is on the left hip. The skirt has no label; the bolduc number on the jacket is 39327.

WOOL MOHAIR HOUNDSTOOTH

12. Photographed for the September 15, 1966, issue of *Vogue*, this straight skirt is fabricated in a wool/mohair houndstooth pattern. It has slot seams on the front. The underlay is black taffeta and shows when the wearer moves. The same fabric is used for the waistband. The skirt appears to have been altered since the waistband is uneven at the opening and the fabric pattern doesn't match. The quilting rows on the skirt are 3$\frac{3}{4}$ in. apart. The skirt has no label; the bolduc number on the jacket is 31590.

13

14

WOOL BOUCLÉ

13. Fabricated in a wool boucle' and lined with a plain-weave silk, this straight skirt is from the early 1960s. The skirt has four gores with two zippers on the back. The unquilted skirt has no darts and is eased to the waistband. The seams on the skirt and lining have been overcast by hand. It appears to be the original length, but the lining has been shortened. The skirt has no label.

VELVET AND SILK

14. Fabricated in wine-colored velvet and lined with silk, this skirt is trimmed with a satin bias binding and rayon lip braid at the waist. The braid is slightly damaged from the hook closure and the white cord inside shows through. The faux wrap is on the skirt back. The overlap is faced with two layers of chiffon; the rest of the lining is plain-weave silk. Although it's unusual, the skirt has a label at center back with its own bolduc number, 50085.

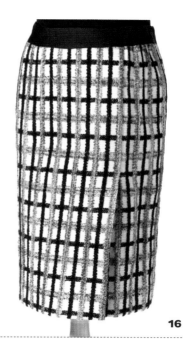

15

16

MOHAIR AND WOOL PLAID

15. From the late 1960s, this straight skirt is cut with 11 panels so the fabric pattern can be arranged attractively. The quilting is on both sides of the gold stripes, and at center front, the center of the red stripe. The waist edge is interfaced with petersham and faced with the silk lining. On the outside, the skirt is stitched 1$\frac{3}{8}$ in. below the edge to simulate a waistband. There is a single zipper on the left hip. The skirt has no label; the bolduc number on the jacket is 36958.

WOOL PLAID

16. From 1967, this stunning faux wrap skirt is matched vertically as well as horizontally. The only trim at the edge of the overlap is the gold stripe on the fabric pattern. The navy silk waistband is 1$\frac{5}{8}$ in. wide; it matches the blouse and is faced with the same material. The quilting rows are spaced 1$\frac{5}{8}$ in. apart and located at the edges of the vertical stripes. The four-gored skirt has no side seams and a single zipper on the left hip. A photo of this suit is included in the book *Chanel: Collections and Creations* by Daniele Bott. The skirt has no label; the bolduc number on the jacket is 33798.

17

18

BROWN TWEED

17. This skirt is from the mid-1970s. At the waist, the skirt lining extends almost to the top of the waistband, and the waistband does not have a separate facing. The top of the lining is sewn by hand with a row of pick stitches 1/2 in. from the edge. The skirt has a label on the lining at the back. This is unusual because couture skirts rarely have a label, but it could be because it was made in a different workroom from the jacket. The bolduc number on the skirt is too faded to read; the number on the jacket is 49779.

WOOL TWEED

18. Fabricated in a wool tweed with a leno weave, this faux wrap is lined with plain-weave silk to the edges. I made the skirt to wear with several black jackets in my wardrobe, so I did not add a trim. There are no side seams, and all darts were replaced by easing. The quilting rows are spaced 2 in. apart. The waistband is finished with a silk lining. At the center back opening, the waistband abuts and is fastened with coat hooks and eyes. Cross-stitches on the inside of the waistband mark the center front.

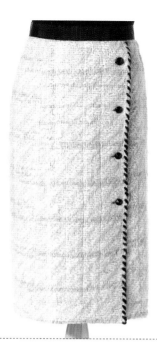

19

20

MOHAIR AND WOOL HOUNDSTOOTH

19. Photographed in *Vogue* (March 15, 1964), this mohair and wool skirt is trimmed with black yarn whipstitched over the edges. The silk gauze lining is quilted to the skirt fabric every 1½ in.; the jacket is quilted every 3 in. The skirt has wraps on both the front and back. This skirt is in very poor condition and has been altered badly. Originally, it was probably a dress with a grosgrain waist stay; the bodice was cut off, leaving only the stay. The skirt has no label; the bolduc number on the jacket is 24313.

WOOL PLAID

20. An early Comeback design from the late 1950s, this skirt is fabricated in the Prince of Wales plaid. Located on the lighter stripes to give the illusion of a smaller waist, darts replace the side seams to shape the skirt. A self-fabric rectangle was inserted on the waistband to lengthen the band to fit a larger figure. There are two zippers on the skirt back, which facilitate dressing and prevent the zipper from showing below the jacket hem. The center back panel has a silk backing to preserve the shape. There is no label on the skirt; the bolduc number on the jacket is 11705.

METRIC EQUIVALENCY CHART

One inch equals approximately 2.54 centimeters. To convert inches to centimeters, multiply the figure in inches by 2.54 and round off to the nearest half centimeter, or use the chart below, whose figures are rounded off (1 centimeter equals 10 millimeters).

⅛ in. = 3 mm	9 in. = 23 cm
¼ in. = 6 mm	10 in. = 25.5 cm
⅜ in. = 1 cm	12 in. = 30.5 cm
½ in. = 1.3 cm	14 in. = 35.5 cm
⅝ in. = 1.5 cm	15 in. = 38 cm
¾ in. = 2 cm	16 in. = 40.5 cm
⅞ in. = 2.2 cm	18 in. = 45.5 cm
1 in. = 2.5 cm	20 in. = 51 cm
2 in. = 5 cm	21 in. = 53.5 cm
3 in. = 7.5 cm	22 in. = 56 cm
4 in. = 10 cm	24 in. = 61 cm
5 in. = 12.5 cm	25 in. = 63.5 cm
6 in. = 15 cm	36 in. = 92 cm
7 in. = 18 cm	45 in. = 114.5 cm
8 in. = 20.5 cm	60 in. = 152 cm

FOR FURTHER READING

Abrams, Dennis. *Coco Chanel*. New York: Chelsea House, 2011.

Baillén, Claude. *Chanel Solitaire*. New York: Quadrangle/New York Times Book Co., 1971.

Ballard, Bettina. *In My Fashion*. New York: David McKay Company, Inc., 1960.

Baudot, François. *Chanel*. New York: Assouline, 2003.

Bott, Daniele. *Chanel: Collections and Creations*. London: Thames and Hudson, 2007.

"Chanel Designs Again." *Vogue*, February 15, 1954, 83–84.

"Chanel: Perennial Direction Maker." *American Fabrics*, Fall/Winter 1963, 7.

Chaney, Lisa. *Coco Chanel: An Intimate Life*. New York: Viking, 2011.

Charles-Roux, Edmonde. *Chanel*. Translated by Nancy Amphoux. London: HarperCollins, 1989.

———. *Chanel and Her World*. London: The Vendome Press, 1979.

———. *The World of Coco Chanel*. London: Thames and Hudson, 2005.

Daves, Jessica. *Ready-Made Miracle: The Story of American Fashion for the Millions*. New York: Putnam, 1967.

De la Haye, Amy. *Chanel*. London: V&A Publishing, 2011.

Delay, Claude (née Baillén). *Chanel Solitaire*. Translated by Barbara Bray. London: Collins, 1973.

Fiemeyer, Isabelle. *Intimate Chanel*. Paris: Flammarion SA, 2011.

Galante, Pierre. *Mademoiselle Chanel*. Translated by E. Geist and J. Wood. Chicago: H. Regnery, 1973.

Gidel, Henry. *Coco Chanel*. Paris: Editions Flammarion, 2000.

Haedrich, Marcel. *Coco Chanel: Her Life, Her Secrets*. Translated by C. L. Markmann. London: Robert Hale, 1972.

Hawes, Elizabeth. *Fashion Is Spinach*. New York: Grosset & Dunlap Publishers, 1940.

Holt, Alexia. *Reviewing Chanel: A Catalogue Raisonné and Critical Survey of the Dress Designs by Chanel Published in British and French Vogue 1916–1929*. Glasgow: University of Glasgow, 1997.

Kennett, Frances. *Coco: The Life and Loves of Gabrielle Chanel*. London: Victor Gollancz Ltd., 1989.

Koda, Harold, and Andrew Bolton. *Chanel*. New York: The Metropolitan Museum of Art, 2005.

"Luxury hidden away in the perfection of detail." *Vogue*, February 15, 1954, 83.

Madsen, Axel. *Coco Chanel: A Biography*. London: Bloomsbury, 1990.

Mazzeo, Tilar J. *The Secret of Chanel No. 5: The Intimate History of the World's Most Famous Perfume*. New York, Harper Collins, 2010.

Morand, Paul. *The Allure of Chanel*. Translated by Euan Cameron. London: Pushkin Press, 2008.

Richards, Melissa. *Chanel: Key Collections*. London: Welcome Rain Publishers, 2000.

Simon, Linda. *Coco Chanel*. London: Reaktion Books, Ltd., 2011.

Steele, Valerie. *Women of Style*. New York: Rizzoli, 1991.

Vaughan, Hal. *Sleeping with the Enemy: Coco Chanel's Secret War*. New York: Alfred A. Knopf, 2011.

Wallach, Janet. *Chanel: Her Style and Her Life*. New York: Nan A. Talese, 1998.

PERIODICALS

Current Biography Yearbook, 1954, 169–171.

Harper's Bazaar, 1954.

Look, October 23, 1962.

New York Times, September 9, 1957, 28.

New York Times, June 12, 1957, 58.

New York Times, November 1, 2012, F9.

The New Yorker, September 28, 1957.

Vogue, 1916–2004.

Vogue, March 15, 1964.

Women's Wear Daily 1919–1993.

RESORCES

UNITED STATES

United States
Apple Annie Fabrics
566 Wilbur Ave.
Swansea, MA 02777
(866) 675-9844
www.appleanniefabrics.com
(fabrics, buttons)

Britex Fabrics
146 Geary St.
San Francisco, CA 94108
(415) 392-2910
www.britexfabrics.com
(fabrics, trims, chain)

David Coffin
1098 Winchuck River Rd.
Brookings, OR 97415
dpcoffin@earthlink.net
www.shaefferonchanel.blogspot.com
(CD The Shaeffer Collection:
Chanel)

Eurosteam Next Generation Iron
Redfern Enterprises
(877) 387-7770
www.redfernent.com
(iron)

LH Design
12741 Iris Way
Eagle River, AK 99577
lhdesign@gci.net
(shoulder stand)

Linton Tweeds Ltd.
Shaddon Mills
Shaddongate
Carlisle, Cumbria
CA2 5TZ
England
44-1228-527-569
www.lintondirect.co.uk

Professional Sewing Supplies
2623 Boylston Ave. E.
Seattle, WA 98102
(206) 324-8823
profsewingsupplies@comcast.net
(basting threads)

Sawyer Brook Distinctive Fabrics
P.O. Box 1800
Clinton, MA 01510
(800) 290-2739
www.sawyerbrook.com
(fabrics, buttons)

Superior Threads
87 E. 2580 S.
St. George, UT 84790
(800) 499-1777
www.superiorthreads.com
(silk threads, thread color chart)

Wawak
1059 Powers Rd.
Conklin, NY 13748
(800) 654-2235
www.wawak.com
(wigan)

ABOUT THE AUTHOR

CLAIRE B. SHAEFFER is an internationally recognized expert in fashion design and construction techniques for haute couture and high-end ready-to-wear. She is a longtime designer for Vogue Patterns, a frequent contributor to *Threads* magazine, and the author of numerous books. Shaeffer served as Couture Sewing Technique Consultant for the Museum of the City of New York's online exhibit "Worth & Mainbocher." She is the recipient of the Association of Sewing & Design Professional's Lifetime Achievement Award and has been inducted into the American Sewing Guild Sewing Hall of Fame.

INDEX

If you like this book, you'll love these bestsellers by Claire B. Shaeffer.

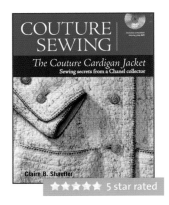
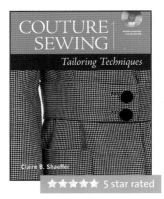
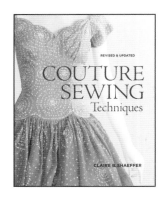

COUTURE
SEWING

The Couture Skirt

CLAIRE B. SHAEFFER

The Taunton Press

The Taunton Press
Inspiration for hands-on living®

The Taunton Press, Inc.
63 South Main Street
PO Box 5506
Newtown, CT 06470-5506
e-mail: tp@taunton.com

Executive editor: Shawna Mullen
Assistant editor: Tim Stobierski
Technical editor: Robin Denning
Copy editor: Betty Christiansen
Indexer: Cathy Goddard
Cover and interior design: Stacy Wakefield Forte
Layout: Susan Lampe-Wilson
Illustrators: Steve Buchanan and Christine Erikson
Photographer (All skirt and skirt details): Liam Goodman
Stylist: Angela Hastings
Video stills/Step-by-step process photos: Gary Junken

The following names/manufacturers appearing in *Couture Sewing: The Couture Skirt* are trademarks: Chanel®, Vogue Patterns®

Library of Congress Cataloging-in-Publication Data
Shaeffer, Claire B.
  Couture sewing : the couture skirt : more sewing secrets from a Chanel collector / Claire B. Shaeffer.
    pages cm
  Includes index.
  ISBN 978-1-62710-387-9
1. Skirts. 2. Tailoring (Women's) I. Title.
  TT540.S364 2014
  687'.044--dc23
                        2014041911

Printed in the United States of America
10 9 8 7 6 5 4 3 2 1

This book is dedicated to everyone, but especially my students, who appreciate fine workmanship and enjoy creating beautiful designs.